THE *honest* ENNEAGRAM

Andrews McMeel Publishing
a division of Andrews McMeel Universal
1130 Walnut Street, Kansas City, Missouri 64106

www.andrewsmcmeel.com

20 21 22 23 24 TEN 10 9 8 7 6 5 4 3 2 1

ISBN: 978-1-5248-5402-7
Library of Congress Control Number: 2019956827

Editor: Katie Gould
Designer: Spencer Williams
Production Editor: Meg Daniels
Production Manager: Tamara Haus

ATTENTION: SCHOOLS AND BUSINESSES
Andrews McMeel books are available at quantity discounts with bulk purchase for educational, business, or sales promotional use. For information, please e-mail the Andrews McMeel Publishing Special Sales Department: specialsales@amuniversal.com.

THE *honest* ENNEAGRAM

KNOW YOUR TYPE
OWN YOUR CHALLENGES
EMBRACE YOUR GROWTH

Sarajane Case

Andrews McMeel
PUBLISHING®

CONTENTS

INTRODUCTION

Being a human is hard. Yet we are never going to graduate from the human experience.

So often I've found myself seeking an end point—a destination of some kind that tells me I've "made it," that I've finally figured out how not to be a person with flaws and aches and blind spots, a transcending of the human experience.

Still, after all of these years, I've found that most of life's turmoil comes from fighting the reality that I am human and life is full of ups and downs and in-betweens. To make it even clearer, the struggles I had as a high schooler are the same struggles I have now. I've spent every single day of my adult and adolescent life focused on being better and doing better, and yet the struggles are the same. Yes, I've learned how to soften them, and yes, I have learned ways to do less harm to myself and others in the process. But I am still the person I've always been. I am still only human.

In fact, it's the moment I think I've surpassed them that I find myself less aware than ever of the way they're impacting me.

What's important is that we wake up each day willing and ready to do the best we can with what we have. Some days, that's not so much, and on others, we shine. Both are OK. Both are normal. All of this is simply human.

This book is all about the Enneagram—a map of human psyche that helps us come face-to-face with our blind spots (the areas of our personality that show up over and over again, often without our full awareness). We ALL have blind spots. No one is beyond having parts of their personality that we aren't one hundred percent aware of. It can feel vulnerable and challenging to look at them and uncomfortable to admit to ourselves—and especially to others.

However, there is a freedom on the other side of knowing our unconscious behavior patterns. It increases our ability to relate to the world from an honest and whole state of mind. This is one of the key steps to full self-acceptance, integrated confidence, and self-trust. It is also one of my favorite cures for impostor syndrome. If you are aware of your blind spots and are proactive in holding space for them, you can't ever be "found out," because you already know.

It was close to five years ago when a friend looked over at me during a bonfire and said, "Have you heard of the Enneagram?" That question changed the trajectory of my life forever.

It kick-started what would be a two-year journey of diving deep into self-discovery. The Enneagram is a system that breaks people up into nine distinct personality types. Each type has a unique fear, motivation, and set of behavior patterns based on those motivations.

I took close to two years to nail down my type, and through that process, I dove deep into the intricacies of each type. I started to see patterns between the Enneagram types and how my consulting clients were engaging in their work lives.

It gave me amazing insight into not only what we are doing but also why we are doing it. As a consultant, I found this tool invaluable. So often, we focus on how to change our habits, but we forget to ask ourselves why those habits are there in the first place. Once we identify what we're trying to accomplish with those habits, we can deal with the root of the issue. This is what the Enneagram made possible for me in my own life and the lives of my clients.

I've spent the last five years consuming every piece of Enneagram-related content available. I read the books, listened to the podcasts, and watched the YouTube channels. When that wasn't enough, I invested in my own Enneagram certification with Integrative Enneagram Solutions based out of South Africa.

In that process, I started a little Instagram account called Enneagram & Coffee. The account started because I was annoying my friends and family with the desire to make everything about the Enneagram. Finally, a friend said, "Just start an Instagram account already." So I did.

Within three days, the account had grown to over 100,000 followers, and it became clear that this is a conversation we're all wanting to have.

I'm not surprised by the attraction to the Enneagram. It's an amazing tool that allows us to fast-track the process of self-discovery. What would normally take many decades to learn through lots of painful trial and error can be read in the description of your Enneagram type, and that is life-altering magic.

I've had the opportunity to support hundreds of thousands of people in the process of working with the Enneagram, and nothing has been as rewarding for me as that has.

I spend time coaching clients on how to use the Enneagram in their businesses, I have a membership community focused on using the Enneagram for personal growth, I speak to large conferences about the work of the Enneagram, and now I'm here writing to you.

I decided to write this book as a way to make the Enneagram easier to digest. So many of the Enneagram books I read were textbook in nature. Long, technical, and overwhelming for beginners. I hope this book feels less like a textbook and more like a really good friend.

It's also important to me that you have not only the information for what your Enneagram type is but also some tools and tips for how to work with your type for growth. That's why I'm sharing the Enneagram elements as well as my coaching method for working with the Enneagram.

I encourage you to read the chapter for your type as well as the chapters applying to friends, family, and coworkers. It can be transformational for your understanding of yourself and can be healing in your understanding of those around you.

MY APPROACH

The Enneagram is, in essence, a theory. It's a series of observations put together over time that make a whole lot of sense. Just like any theory, there are several schools of thought in the world of the Enneagram.

You might hear Claudio Naranjo say one thing, while Helen Palmer or Richard Rohr says another. They mostly play together pretty well, and then sometimes they contradict one another.

When I came to the Enneagram, I had a background in creative consulting and expertise in self-compassionate productivity. I built my business helping people get their creative work out into the world while being very, very kind to themselves in the process.

When I began studying the Enneagram, I saw a lot of language that I would never use with a client, or even with myself—words like "lazy" or "gluttonous," words that imply a fatal flaw which has no rhyme or reason behind it.

I began researching the reasons that people may seem "lazy" or "dramatic" based on their type patterns. Often, when a type seems "lazy," those people are actually just tired from spending the entire day pleasing other people. When they seem "dramatic," they feel like if they just expressed themselves well enough, you'd understand them to the degree that they crave to be known. With this realization, I approached all of the elements of the Enneagram through a new lens. I broke them apart and asked one simple question: "How can I view this with more compassionate understanding?"

Here's what I've found over my years as a consultant—you cannot shame someone into being a better version of themselves. Instead, we all need a mixture of consistency paired with compassionate understanding.

You see, most of us have spent our entire lives fixated on what we could be doing differently and laser-focused on all the things that are wrong with us. We spend years of our lives trying to discipline ourselves to change. Yet we find ourselves dealing with the same issues ten, twenty, or thirty years later. The reason for this is that growth isn't a destination. We won't wake up one day with the exact personality that we want, the perfect life, and no visible conflict. That place does not exist.

In fact, I challenge you to consider that the struggles you deal with now may be the struggles you deal with for the rest of your life. (Some of you thought about burning this book just now). You may soften your response to them over time and find healthier ways to deal with them. But the relationship to the struggle doesn't end. And that's why it's important that you remember in this work that growth isn't a destination—it's a relationship. It's waking up every single day and choosing to interact with the world in a way that does less harm to yourself and others and adds more beauty to the world.

How do you do that? I work with the H.O.N.E.S.T. method. It's a system that I designed for myself and my clients to have a healthy, loving, and productive relationship with our lives. I break it down for you on page 17.

I pair this method with the elements of the Enneagram to support myself, my relationships, and my businesses, and to help my clients do the same. That's the work we'll be doing together in this book. I will walk through each Enneagram type and, using the H.O.N.E.S.T. method, help you create a healthy, loving, and productive relationship with your life!

Soon I will go through each of the steps of the method with you in detail, but let's first make sure we're caught up on the elements of the Enneagram itself. Even if you are familiar with it, I encourage you to read through this section. It will help put the rest of the chapters into context.

ELEMENTS OF THE ENNEAGRAM

Like I mentioned earlier, the Enneagram is a theory of personality based on decades of observation, oral tradition, and research. It provides us with nine distinct profiles of people who have the same motivations and fears and, therefore, often have a lot of the same behavior patterns.

Learning the Enneagram is a bit like learning Photoshop. You figure out one element and you think you have it all nailed down, and then you learn a little more and then a little more, and you realize that the learning may never end. (That's kind of what I love about the Enneagram, if we're being honest.)

With that being said, every book you read on the Enneagram and every school you study will share different elements of the Enneagram or different approaches to working with it. Below are the elements I choose to work with, and my approach to working with them all, in the service of compassionate understanding.

SUBTYPES

Each Enneagram type has three distinct instinctual variants that we call "subtypes." Essentially, this is the way that we create distinction in personality patterns among people of the same type. We each have all three of these variants within us; however, we usually have one that is dominant. This dominant variant adds a level of distinction around what motivates us and how that shows up in the world.

The three variants are:

Sexual. This subtype is much less exciting than the name implies. The sexual subtype is focused on one-to-one connections. They prefer deeper connection and intense contact. While this may mean seeking out that connection with a potential mate, it can also mean looking for intensity of experiences. Often, those with sexual subtypes can recognize themselves because they spend a significant amount of their time looking for the person that will complete them.

Self-preservation. This subtype is focused on physical safety and comfort. These people may find themselves worried about their needs, such as housing, food, money, or health. Often, self-preservation subtypes can recognize themselves because they spend a significant amount of their time focused on what will make them the most comfortable in their environment.

Social. This subtype isn't necessarily extroverted or the life of the party. Instead, it speaks more to the person's desire to be liked. Social subtypes are focused on how people are responding to them and whether they are in good standing with the group. Often, social subtypes can recognize themselves because they spend a significant amount of their time aware of how they are being received by others.

WINGS

"Wings" in the Enneagram refers to the two types on either side of your dominant type, meaning that we have access to much of what drives and motivates the adjacent types. For example, a type one has access to facets of both type nine and type two. In most people, one wing presents as dominant, an added distinction to their type. However, we all have access to the strengths and weaknesses of both of our wings.

When studying subtypes and wings, I like seeing the diagram as a color wheel. Each Enneagram type is a different color, and the subtypes and wings offer us shades of that color. For instance, if type three is blue, then a social 3w4 is more like indigo.

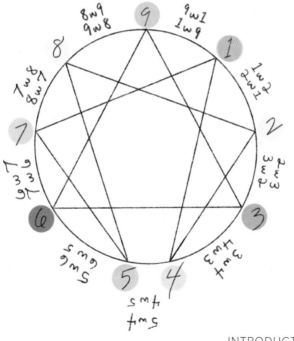

LINES

This is perhaps one of the coolest pieces of the Enneagram, and one of the things that we can really engage with on a day-to-day basis. Each type has two lines drawn to and from it. One line represents where that type goes in stress, and the other line represents where that type goes in rest.

You can grow up either of those lines to access the high levels of health in that type, or you can slip down either of those lines to the low levels of health in that type.

When stressed, we may find that we are showing symptoms of the low levels of health of the type that we move toward in stress. To remedy that stress, we can pull from the high levels of our rest type.

For example, a type seven who is stressed may become perfection-istic or judgmental (like the lower levels of a type one). To relieve that stress and bring in a bit of self-care, type sevens can pull from the higher levels of type five, taking time to research in-depth things they care about, enjoying time to themselves, intentionally managing their energy levels, etc.

When we are a bit too comfortable in our lives with little stress, strain, or conflict, we may find ourselves going numb to our existence—forgetting to pour energy into things that matter to us or settling for a life that doesn't really serve our highest good. In these times, we may exhibit some of the lower levels of the type we move toward in rest. To help us, we can pull from the higher levels of our stress type.

For instance, that same type seven could slip into isolation, shutting people out and flaking on plans in favor of projects he or she is work-ing on. To remedy this, the type seven can take from the higher levels of type one by creating structure, routine, and consistency, so they can finish projects and follow through with commitments.

LEVELS OF HEALTH

Each type has a range of health, from "unhealthy" to "average" to "healthy." Think of the levels like this:

We may experience a range of health in a given day. We could wake up feeling like the highest version of ourselves. Later in the day, however, we could be triggered and end up expressing the lower levels of our type. When working with the levels, I think of it as a dance of awareness. Own what you're capable of, know what is normal, and set yourself up to exhibit the higher levels of what is available to you.

I am personally very put off by hearing the phrase "a healthy two" or "an unhealthy two." When we start describing people as healthy or unhealthy, we are not only shaming them in their process but also robbing them of their own relationship to this process. We are all on the journey together, doing the best we can each day with what we've been given.

THE H.O.N.E.S.T. METHOD

Do you want to know the thing that has positively impacted my life more than anything else? It's not work ethic or connections or even self-care. In fact, I think it may surprise you. The thing that has impacted my life for the better in every single way is my ability to admit to myself and others that I am sometimes the worst.

I don't mean that I shame myself or live in guilt. I mean that I stare at my worst traits, and I hold them lightly. I own that I bring things to the table that aren't always helpful, and I let that impact the way I move through the world.

That awareness brings me the clarity I need to know how to grow my business, create healthy relationships, take care of my body and heart, and create from a place of inspiration.

Knowing where I fall short allows me to create a support plan. It allows others to feel comfortable and safe in my presence. It actually helps me do less harm to people who enter my path. However, the only reason that this works is because I started with a deep well of self-love. I learned to love myself no matter what. I learned that unconditional acceptance of who I am comes from the ability to celebrate my strengths and accept my weaknesses. This process has changed everything for me.

We are all worthy of full self-acceptance, and I believe that full self-acceptance starts with being honest. It's not honest to pretend we don't have flaws. It's also not honest to pretend we don't have strengths. True, honest, deep self-love requires our ability to hold both.

My dear, you are so worthy of it all—full, deep, rich self-acceptance for exactly who you are. No excuses and no apologies.

This is the method I use both in my own Enneagram work and the work I do with clients. It's allowed me to research the Enneagram and turn it into actionable growth steps. Let's talk in-depth about what having an H.O.N.E.S.T. relationship with yourself means.

HONOR YOUR STRENGTHS

This is step one. This is the foundation of everything else that we are doing here. I need you to hold tightly to the fact that you, just like everyone else, are incredible. You're remarkable. Truly. All of the tiny intricate details that make you up are beyond awe-inspiring.

I want you to get to the point where you can say, "I'm so proud of myself for . . ." without apologizing, without wincing, without doing that thing we do where we say some of the words really quiet because we think that makes them less present.

In order to have an honest relationship with yourself, you must first support that with not only self-acceptance but also self-delight.

Think of it this way: how would it feel if you were in a relationship with a person who had never complimented you, and when the person did compliment you, he or she was uncomfortable? However, the person did start going in on all of the things you needed to work on. Would you feel safe there? Would you take the person's feedback and make positive changes in your life? No! You would shrivel up into a ball of self-loathing or, hopefully, break up with that person ASAP.

You can't do the work of growth until you first develop a safe place to land.

OPEN YOUR EYES TO BLIND SPOTS

We all know someone who tries to pretend they don't have anything to fix. You watch them complain about their life over and over again, and it seems clear to you that if they just changed x, y, and z, they'd be fine. But most people are terrified to look at their darkness.

I was speaking to a woman at the end of a conference recently and she said, "It's a 'monster-in-the-closet' situation." And she's totally right. We think it's so scary, so we freak out and hide from it, and we let it take up a ton of brain space while we also, quite frankly, ignore it. Yet, what happens when we open the closet? We find out that the "monster" was actually just a broom. Not exactly pretty, but not terrifying either.

The more we can look into our darkness, the easier it is for us to deal with it. Remember, this is an ongoing process. We are building a relationship with life that is rich, fulfilling, and kind. Getting honest with your blind spots and the things you use to cope will allow you to walk through the world doing less harm to yourself and others.

NOTE YOUR SUPPORT PLAN

One of the biggest mistakes I see my clients make is that they try to get the results they want using the tactics of someone else. When they inevitably fail, instead of questioning if it was the tactics that didn't serve them, they berate themselves for being "failures" or give up and lose interest. The Enneagram shines a big bright spotlight on why this approach doesn't work.

We are all different, and we all have unique motivations and fears that drive our daily habits. Get intimate with the motivations of your type so that you can truly know why you want the things you want, and develop a plan to achieve them that takes YOU into consideration.

EXPLORE YOUR RELATIONSHIPS

As we explore our contribution to relationships, it's important that we start by deeply accepting the reality that we can't rush the growth of others. It is so very tempting to try to get the people in our lives to behave how we want them to. I get asked all the time, "How do I get my type X partner to __?" There's nothing wrong with the question, and there are certainly ways to engage with other types that help us feel seen and help them feel seen as well. However, we have to be careful not to use the Enneagram as a tool to get what we want from the people in our lives without vulnerability and without looking at ourselves first.

First and foremost, our work with the Enneagram is looking at ourselves, owning our own blind spots and worldview. It is shockingly easy to shift our focus to how other people in our lives aren't showing up in the ways we think they should or even doing the work in the way we think they should. This can be a distraction from the beautiful work that is available to you.

Start exploring what you bring to the table, both positively and negatively, in the relationships in your life. The Enneagram does a great job of laying this out for us, and I will share specifics later for each type. However, you can likely already start to think of behavior patterns you have in your life.

SOFTEN YOUR PATH

We all have habits that simply aren't serving us. The Enneagram shines light on those vividly.

There are self-help gurus out there teaching that the path to growth and change is simply to focus more, to keep going even when it sucks, to buy more products, and to just be better.

And I couldn't disagree more.

Personal growth isn't about discipline; it's about understanding and making micro-shifts to be closer to who you want to be. It's about the relationship.

I used to think that my lack of progress meant that I just wasn't trying hard enough or, honestly, that I was a failure. If I could just discipline myself enough, then I would be worthy of the good things I wanted in my life.

It wasn't until I decided to stop FORCING myself into someone else's definition of "good" that I felt the freedom to truly start making shifts in my life.

It wasn't until I quit disciplining myself that I was able to take HUGE steps in my personal and professional lives. I learned something that no one else was teaching—a clear-cut approach to personal growth, self-confidence, and creative expression that had nothing to do with shame and guilt.

Instead, it's about curiosity and habit-shifting. It's about focusing on how you operate and why something isn't working for you, and making micro-adjustments that serve you better. It's about taking the conversation from "Just be better" to "What do you need to feel supported in this process?" and then setting small, achievable goals to build a new habit.

As mentioned earlier, certain schools of the Enneagram describe the struggles of each type with language that I find shaming and, quite frankly, unhelpful. An example of this is calling type nines "lazy." Here's how we can use this process with our type nines:

The Path of Discipline

I watch more TV than I'd like to

That means I'm lazy

I should wake up at 5 a.m. tomorrow and workout

Hits snooze button and misses workout

"I'm so lazy."

The Path of Curiosity

"I watch more TV than I would like to."

Why do I watch TV?

I'm too tired to do anything else

Why am I so tired?

I spent all day thinking about other people's needs and trying to make them happy

What would it feel like if tomorrow I did my best to not give my energy away to other people

TURN THAT INTO SOMETHING BEAUTIFUL

I believe that we are all creative and we all need to create. That doesn't mean that we are all artists or painters. I mean we all have creative ways to express ourselves that need to be explored. Maybe for you that's writing or dancing or knitting. It doesn't have to be big, and it doesn't have to be public. It just has to be pulling something out of you in a new and engaging way.

When we create, we breathe new life into our days, we contribute to the world, we increase our sense of pride in who we are, and we can use what we make to show love to the people in our lives. If those reasons don't do it for you, studies have shown that creating can actually reduce stress and anxiety and temper mood swings.

You have something beautiful to share and we are all better off when you share it.

In this work, I hope that you find a dance with life, a way to walk through the world that offers ease and understanding. My hope is that you find out and celebrate that you are truly remarkable, you are not any more special or flawed than anyone else, and you are also sometimes your own worst enemy.

I hope when you acknowledge the areas that need some massaging that you don't beat yourself up over it. I hope you take the time to understand why you operate the way you do and gently step into new ways of behaving.

I hope you can end the cycle of discipline and shame and move into a new sustainable relationship to personal growth that starts with compassionate curiosity.

I know that there are people who think beginning a relationship with yourself is selfish, narcissistic, and a waste of time. But I'm telling you that it's the key to everything. This is the path to making the impact you are trying to create. This is the way to live a life you love without hating yourself or sacrificing your values along the way. This is how you positively impact the lives of others. Don't hold back from a loving, healthy, and honest relationship with who you are. To me, that's much more selfish and does much more harm.

TRIGGER WARNING

This book isn't here to beat you over the head with the things you don't like about yourself. In fact, it's here to do the opposite. I want to warn you of two possible reactions you could have to reading about your type pattern:

1. It could sting.
It's uncomfortable to read your type laid out on a page. It feels weird to be seen in your shadow. It's important to remember that you aren't only the lower levels of your type. You are capable of all of the good too. That's why I want you to focus on honoring your strengths first. Give them their time in the sun. That will help you remember that shadow and light play together, and we can't have one without the other.

2. You may hear one thing when I'm saying another.
I see this happen all the time on my Instagram account. I say something like, "Type fives need a lot of time alone to recharge." And I get messages from type fives saying things like, "Why do you always call us lazy?" "Why do you think all type fives are hermits who never leave their houses?" "Have you ever even met a type five? We have friends and are social!"

It's important to remember that we have a lot of voices in our heads: parents, partners, teachers, friends, and even books, whose words can plant little seeds of shame and doubt and have us latching onto ideas of who we are. Sometimes we hold these ideas and believe them, and other times we do everything in our power to fight against them. In both cases, it can be easy to interpret the world through the lens of what we already believe.

It can be tempting to interpret this book through the wounds that you already carry. I'm so sorry that you carry those burdens, but I want you to know that I am saying exactly what I mean here—no extra intentions are hiding between the lines, no notes of judgment or shame or guilt-tripping reside secretly in the paper.

You are safe here and I want the best for you.

EXPLORE YOUR TYPE

MORALIST

REFORMER

PERFECTIONIST

CHAMPION OF GOOD

Type One

*"Most of my life I've believed that I'll be OK
if I just do the right thing."*

BINGO

"Why did you load the dishwasher like that?"	Organizes for fun	"It's almost ready, just not quite right yet . . ."	"I could really be better at . . ."	"You could really be better at . . ."
Thorough AF.	Thinks accomplishing things is rest	Lists.	Day planners.	"Why wouldn't you just follow the rules?"
"Where's your blinker, buddy?"	Things are black and white—right or wrong.	1	Routines are life.	"Am I a bad person?"
"It would be so much better if you just . . ."	Justice.	Lives with a strong moral compass	Podcasts while cleaning	Donates to causes that are important to them.
Intense inner critic.	"Why did you bring that into my house?"	"I'm not angry, I'm just disappointed."	A genuinely good person.	Finds every typo

SELF-CARE CHECK-IN

By Enneagram type.

1 - IF YOU WERE SAFE TO BE 100% HONEST ABOUT THE WAY YOU FEEL, WHAT WOULD YOU ACKNOWLEDGE AND HOW WOULD YOU EXPRESS YOURSELF?

2 - WHERE DO YOU FEEL RESENTMENT? IS THERE A BOUNDARY THERE THAT NEEDS TO BE SET?

3 - WHEN IS THE LAST TIME YOU JUST HAD FUN WITHOUT A REASON BEHIND IT?

4 - CAN YOU TAKE A MOMENT TO FOCUS ON WHAT IS INCREDIBLE ABOUT YOU & YOUR LIFE?

5 - WHEN IS THE LAST TIME YOU TOOK A LEISURLEY WALK?

6 - IF YOU WERE COMPLETELY LOYAL TO YOUR OWN VISION FOR LIFE, WHAT WOULD CHANGE TODAY?

7 - ARE YOU ESCAPING INTO THE FUTURE TODAY? CAN YOU TAKE SOME TIME TO BE FULLY PRESENT WITH WHAT IS GOOD IN THE HERE & NOW?

8 - ARE YOU BURNING THE CANDLE AT BOTH ENDS? WHERE ARE YOU MAKING THINGS HARDER THAN THEY HAVE TO BE?

9 - WHEN IS THE LAST TIME YOU TOOK INTENTIONAL ACTION TOWARD YOUR GOALS? WHAT'S ONE SMALL ACTION STEP YOU CAN TAKE TODAY?

@enneagramandcoffee

ABOUT TYPE ONE

Basic Desire: "I want to be a good person, to have balance, to live in my integrity."

Basic Fear: "I'm afraid of being a bad person, of being evil or corrupt."

Type ones are disciplined, discerning, and judicious. They learned somewhere along the way that the world is corrupt, and it's their duty to always do the right thing as a way to mend things. They tend to view the world in black and white, right and wrong, and strongly value fairness, justice, and order. Type ones reject their natural impulse toward pleasure, sometimes even if the pleasure is a victimless enjoyment. There's almost a natural rejection of the animalistic side of being human. An impulse may rise up inside of the type one, only to be held inside and ultimately repressed.

Type ones are hardworking, honest, refining, organized, structured, and likely the best people you know.

I chose the title "Champion of Good" for type ones because that's exactly what I believe our type ones do. They show us what it means to live with integrity, be the best version of ourselves, and look for what could be better in our society. They are in constant pursuit of goodness, and we are all better for knowing them.

Most type ones spend a lot of their time and energy in conversation with their inner critic. It's a voice that we all have, but for type ones it's just a bit louder and maybe a bit harsher. The voice tells them that they're always falling short and points out all the ways in which things could be better.

Most type ones confuse this voice for logic and reason. There's a belief that it's the "right" voice and that ignoring it would mean ignoring the truth. The trouble is that giving all of your trust to this voice means no rest for type ones. They could easily spend their lives constantly perfecting everything, which we know is ultimately unachievable. Life is imperfect and so are we, and so are the ones we love.

When we seek constant perfection, we are committing ourselves to a life of constant dissatisfaction.

I believe the hardest thing about being a type one is coming to grips with the elements of being human. When reading the characteristics of their type, it's not uncommon for type ones to feel the heat of shame. A lot of type ones feel that it's "wrong" to be a type one. When you spend so much of your life truly and honestly trying to be the best person you can be, reading this description can feel like you aren't doing a good enough job, which can feel isolating and defeating.

I think it's particularly important for type ones to absorb that every single type has good and bad and in-between. We are all out here trying our best with what we have available to us. You've been working so hard, and this is here to help you find a way to ease into harnessing those strengths while also releasing the expectation that you have to be the one to fix the brokenness that you see all around you.

SUBTYPES OF TYPE ONE

The following subtypes of type one are based on the three instinctual variants and how they interact with the type one's relationship to perfecting. The self-preservation type one turns that desire for perfection inward, attempting to do everything the "right way;" the social type one focuses on being the perfect example of societal standards; and the sexual type one focuses outward on perfecting others.

SELF-PRESERVATION
- Constant worrying and anxiety
- Focused primarily on striving for perfection
- Decent, kind, and gentle person
- Feels a desperate desire to have control over his or her own life
- Attempts to predict the future
- Can look like a type six

SOCIAL
- Takes on the role of the "example" for the right way to be
- Rigid and inflexible
- Non-adaptable
- Confident view of right and wrong
- Desire to be superior
- Often feels alienated in groups of people

SEXUAL
- Focuses on reforming others and not as focused on refining themselves
- Rigid and inflexible
- Can be impatient
- Goes for what they want
- Zealous
- Doesn't often question self
- Can experience "trapdoor" behavior—saying one thing to the world while secretly doing the opposite

TYPE ONE AND WINGS

As a type one, you can pull from either of your wings to help round out your personality. You may find that you already lean in one direction more than the other. However, you have access to the skills and vices of both wings. Here are some qualities you can borrow from your neighbors:

TYPE TWO WING

With this wing, you can increase your empathy game by pulling in the power of warmth and action and the skill of persuasion. You can tap into this wing to take your beliefs to the street and start putting movement behind what you believe. You can rally people to a cause, to volunteer, and to make a difference.

TYPE NINE WING

With this wing, you can start to see things from alternate perspectives. You can place yourself in the shoes of other people and understand where they may be coming from. Finally, tapping into this wing can really aid in flexing your wisdom and consideration muscles and starting to share your perspective from a balanced and understanding perspective.

TYPE ONE AND LINES

When in stress, the type one moves to type four, and when in rest, they move to type seven. With that understanding, here's what you may want to keep in mind in your relationship to stress and self-care.

RECOGNIZING YOUR STRESS

When stressed out, type ones can feel like no one notices how hard they are working and that others don't understand them. They may escape to a place of fantasy—imagining a life different from their own and developing a "grass is greener" internal dialogue.

SELF-CARE INFUSION

When you start to feel this way, you have the tools you need to care for yourself. Use the high side of type seven to support you and relieve the stress that you are carrying. To do this, you can tap into the free-spirited and spontaneous side of yourself. At some point, you learned that being childlike and playful wasn't allowed, so you stuffed those desires deep inside. However, type ones, when they tap into it, can be one of the most playful types on the Enneagram. I recommend that type ones schedule regular times to play "hooky." Give yourself a break from constant perfecting and just exist and play, and surround yourself with things and people who make you laugh.

RECOGNIZING STAGNATION

In the same way that you can use the spontaneity of type seven intentionally, you can also use it by accident. Type ones can be overburdened by responsibilities (often self-inflicted) that can weigh them down and drain their life force. Many times, this can cause type ones to reach a breaking point where they feel resentful, and they may start "acting out" as a form of rebellion. They can develop secret indulgences or drop the ball on obligations as a way to make up for all of the impulses they've been rejecting.

MOTIVATION INFUSION

This is where it's helpful to bring in the high side of type four. Allow yourself to be self-reflecting and aware. Seek out creative ways to express yourself. Get honest with your feelings and what you need. Spend conscious time alone doing things that inspire you.

LEVELS OF HEALTH

HEALTHY

In their healthiest state, type ones are able to let go of the belief that they are in the position to judge. They are able to achieve their desire to be good by becoming wise, open, and accepting and living fully in their integrity.

AVERAGE

In most cases, our type ones are quick to take a stance on "right and wrong" and then work hard to live up to their own high standards. Because they are working so hard to do the "right" thing, they can find themselves resentful when others don't live up to their standards either.

UNHEALTHY

Type ones may become overly restrictive with themselves and others. This is ultimately unsustainable and often causes them to develop hypocritical behavior patterns—condemning behavior publicly while participating in it privately. Eventually that feeling of doing the "wrong" thing can be too much for a type one, and they may begin to feel as if they deserve to be punished.

GETTING H.O.N.E.S.T. FOR TYPE ONE

I imagine if you are a type one reading this, you feel a bit like you've been put through the ringer at this point. I think type ones may have the hardest time of anyone with the Enneagram. That's because you are working so hard every single day to be the best that you can be, and it feels a bit like being told it wasn't good enough. I'm going to ask you to stick with me, though. The next few sections are where the magic of putting this into practice lives, and if anyone is capable of putting this into practice, it's definitely you. Let's take all of the information we just learned and put it together into practical action steps for living out a healthy relationship with yourself.

HONOR YOUR STRENGTHS

The first step is to take time to get really honest with yourself about what makes you amazing. Celebrate all of the elements of your personality that you love. If it's tricky for you to think of things you love about yourself, consider what you do and who you are that contributes positively to the world around you.

A few things that are amazing about type ones:
- You are organized.
- You are hardworking.
- You are honest.
- You are aware of the needs in the world.
- You make things better.
- You help others to want to be better people.
- You are generous.
- You are prepared.
- You are dedicated.
- You are discerning.
- You are a good person.

It's important that you know the goal isn't to avoid being a type one. You don't need to reject everything that you are—even your strengths. It's simply about holding the awareness for what is keeping you away from your essence. It's OK that your good qualities are part of your type pattern—it doesn't make them less good.

Take some time to write out your personal strengths below.

_____

_____

_____

_____

_____

OPEN YOUR EYES TO BLIND SPOTS

This can be particularly strange for type ones because you've spent so much of your life focused on where you are falling short, but most type ones don't consider that the area to work on. Before we dive into your blind spots, I want you to give yourself full permission to not "fix" yourself. It can be easy to overburden yourself with things to work on when you're already working on so much. Take some time not trying to fix who you are. Consider that we are all human and that you're allowed to just exist for a moment. In that moment, read through this section. Allow yourself to hold space for things you actually could be releasing.

A few things to keep in mind as a type one:

1. Your inner critic isn't the authority of right and wrong.
It's not uncommon for type ones to treat their inner critics as a kind of parental figure in their minds—someone who knows best and is telling them when they've succeeded and when they've failed miserably. The trouble is that the inner critic isn't the true voice of right and wrong. It's helpful to create division between yourself and that voice. Give it a name, an identity, or draw a picture of what it looks like, and have conversations with it where you are the authority and it is simply someone who is commenting on your life without your permission. When doing this work, it can be difficult to release the inner critic and you may fear that without constant watching you could fall into bad behavior. However, the truth is that this relationship often leads type

ones toward depression, anxiety, and shame of self. You can trust yourself. You've gotten this far, and that voice isn't serving you.

2. De-prioritizing pleasure doesn't serve you long-term.

A lot of type ones seek constant control over their environment and desire to make sure that everything will be good. This can look like work first and play second. The trouble is that sometimes the play never comes. This would be fine except that when this goes on for too long, it can lead to resentment that comes out in unexpected ways. De-prioritizing pleasure can lead to irritability with loved ones and co-workers, inflexibility, and secret pleasures that are excessive, indulgent, or even illegal. The secret pleasures cause shame, and the one who is working so hard to be good then feels the need for punishment, creating stricter rules that only lead to more resentment, which feeds the desire to act out in secret ways.

The remedy for this is to proactively seek out pleasure. Make sure that you are prioritizing fun and play. Schedule it into your life on a regular basis.

A type one client of mine learned the hard way that postponing pleasure wasn't serving her. After years of overworking and underplaying, she ended up in a coma for four days after experiencing stress-induced cardiac arrest. This moment taught her not just to work but also play—that it doesn't matter what we accomplish or how "right" we are in doing things if we aren't around to enjoy it.

3. Your way isn't the only way.

Often, type ones walk through the world with a strict view of right and wrong and an idea of what it means when someone is "trying" or when they aren't. One of the greatest lessons that a type one can learn is that ALL people are doing the best they can with what they've been given.

I'll pause here for you to breathe because I know that's a direct contradiction to your worldview.

It's true, though. You are doing the best you can with what you know. The person who was rude to the waiter was doing the best he could in that moment with his resources—how little they may have been at the time. All people are born into different circumstances and pick up different tools and tricks and skills along the way. They also pick up trauma and pain and fear. When we operate at our lower levels, we aren't choosing to be the worst version of ourselves. We are simply doing the best we can in that moment with what we have access to.

Viewing the world through this lens can release you of the need to police the people around you. They are doing the best they can with what they have and the things they're prioritizing, and they aren't wrong for it.

It's OK to be human. It can be hard for type ones to admit their humanity. Life for most type ones is a constant race to beating the fact that they and the world are inevitably flawed. Yet, here we all are. Each and every one of us makes mistakes every single day. Sometimes those mistakes lead us to hurt other people, cost our company money, or inconvenience someone else.

When those things happen, it can be hard for type ones to handle the criticism that comes their way. I believe the reason for this isn't that type ones are trying to dodge responsibility for their actions. I truly believe it's because they are trying so hard already that any more "work" on their plate or things to fix about themselves feels over-whelming and disheartening.

In order to take criticism well, our type ones need to release the constant need to perfect unnecessary areas. Get really honest with yourself about where you are expending energy unnecessarily, that could be going into the relationships that you want to preserve or the projects that are most important to you.

It can seem unnatural to prioritize your energy in this way. However, once you start to notice it, you can see how you are giving everything in your life equal weight—treating the re-organization of your computer desktop with the same perfecting weight as you do the person who is asking you to consider how you've hurt their feelings.

4. Find healthy ways to express your anger.
Type ones are in the anger triad of the Enneagram. This means that your primary fixation is around the emotion of anger. However, type ones do this by constantly rejecting their anger. This can turn into irritability, being overly sweet to those you feel anger toward, or even embracing "secret sins."

In order to prevent your anger from coming out sideways, it's impor-tant that you access your relationship to anger on a daily or weekly basis. Develop a practice that allows you to honestly release your anger. Whether that is throwing plates against a wall, taking up boxing, going for a run to heavy metal music, or my suggestion—simply write down everything you're angry about right now. Brain-dump it all on a piece of paper. Get it out fully and then burn it or throw it away. Do this journaling practice each morning for a week and see how you feel!

NOTE YOUR SUPPORT PLAN

This is the part of the process where we get to talk about finding what actually serves YOU when it comes to creating a life you love. This is very exciting for me to share with type ones because, so often, type ones get caught up in doing things the "right" way. That gets a little muddy for us to parse out because, for most type ones, the "right" way seems like the way that works for them.

So, how do we distinguish between what feels like the "right" thing and what is actually going to serve you living your happiest, healthiest, most true-to-your-essence life? For our type ones, I say to start with this simple question: "Does this open me up to being more accepting, open, and relaxed?"

Those specific feelings are symbols that you are in your healthiest state as a type one.

A few things that may support you in the process of opening:
- Listen to podcasts or read books that push you toward more openness.
- Reward a long day by scheduling in time to play.
- Pick up a hobby that isn't work-related and make sure it doesn't become a chore.
- Pair your holistic practices with something practical (e.g., do a walking meditation, listen to a mindfulness podcast while you drive to work, etc.).
- Develop a relationship to non-attachment. Let it breathe, though— don't try to perfect non-attachment. Simply get curious about it and see what happens.
- Perform loving-kindness meditations.
- Listen intentionally when people share thoughts that are in direct contradiction to what you believe.

- When frustrated with someone for not doing things the "right" way, ask yourself why people may do things the way they do.
- Separate your inner critic from yourself. Give the critic a name and an identity and talk to it. Remind it that YOU get to decide what is best for you.
- Get messy! Pick up a hobby or spend the afternoon making a mess. Whether that's potting plants, flinging paint onto a canvas, playing in the rain, etc. Just feel the freedom in releasing control.
- Perform daily brain dumps that acknowledge your anger and honor its right to exist.

What can you do this week to bring in more openness, relaxation, and acceptance? Go ahead and schedule it!

EXPLORE YOUR RELATIONSHIPS

So far, you've honored your strengths, gotten really honest with yourself about your blind spots, and set aside a plan of support in the process. Now it's time to talk about relationships. It's all well and good to do all of this work on our own, but what do we do when someone else comes in and disrupts our perfect synchronicity of self-compassion? This is where we get to explore what you bring into your relationships. What do you positively contribute? What do you do that doesn't serve your work to being the open, wise, discerning, honest, and good human being that you are designed to be?

Beautiful things that type ones bring to their relationships:
- Showing us what it looks like to live honorably.
- Keeping us on task.
- Reminding us to be a good person.
- Giving great advice.
- Generosity.

- Looking out for the well-being of others.
- Reminding us to stay committed to ourselves.
- Consistency and reliability.

A few things that may not be serving your relationships:
- Insisting on knowing the "right" way.
- Trusting only yourself to do things correctly.
- Overburdening yourself with tasks and then resenting people in your life for not doing the same.
- Not deciding where to pick your battles.
- Repressing your anger instead of communicating it directly. (Communicating your anger allows for it to come out thoughtfully and intentionally instead of sideways and sloppy.)
- Nit-picking the people you care about instead of appreciating them as a whole.

The reason we're talking about this—even if it's uncomfortable and sometimes painful—is because in the long run it will bring you so much relief. Holding the truth that both of these lists exist simultaneously is the key to ease in your relationships. Knowing what you can control and what isn't yours to worry about can be extremely relaxing.

That tiny list up there, that's it. Think about that! You are doing so much right!

Take a few minutes to think about your own lists. Write down what you personally bring to your relationships, both positively and negatively.

Now, take a few moments here to think of the three most important relationships in your life. Write out how you would like for them to feel. How would they change if you could imagine a world where they were exactly as you hoped?

What about your lists would need to shift in order to have the relationships that you want?

SOFTEN YOUR PATH

OK, so we've established what makes you amazing. (Way to go, by the way!) We've covered what areas of your life may be in need of some tender love and care. We've even discussed how to support yourself in this growth. Let's now talk about how we're going to keep this process from becoming a straitjacket of self-discipline—because I know you're tempted.

I want to give you these three soft internal shifts to make. Just three things to hold onto each and every day that will help you in the work of being your healthiest type one self.

1. Get curious.

One of the places I would start shifting in yourself is adding more curiosity. Ask "why" much more often—for example, "Why would they do it that way?" or "Why do I feel irritated right now?" This will allow you to find more understanding of the differences in other people and of your own worldview.

Also, explore what things would feel like with curiosity. "How would it feel if I just rested into this?" "How can I show myself more grace in this moment?" "What's the worst thing that could happen if I take four things off of my to-do list today?" Asking this final question keeps you from adding to your list of things to perfect and allows you to simply create a relationship with yourself where you are actually being heard.

2. Redefine "good" for yourself.

This is something every single type one needs to do, especially after learning about the Enneagram. Sit down and read the high levels of health for your type. Then, write out a list of morals for yourself. What do you believe it means to be a good person with this new set of information? Who do you want to be?

3. Prioritize play.
If you take nothing else away from this section, I hope that you hold on to this one. Make play a daily part of your life! Schedule it if you have to, but don't lose track of your lightness. Trying to reason your way to openness and acceptance could happen, but it will take much, much longer than if you open yourself up to enjoying your life more. Integrate play into your day-to-day so that you don't feel resentful long-term and need to force play in to the detriment of something else.

TURN THAT INTO SOMETHING BEAUTIFUL
Creativity is important for all types. However, it's uniquely important for you as a type one. Creativity is one of the quickest ways for you to relax. It can help you get in touch with the true essence of who you are and create the openness of spirit that helps you quickly access your highest self. No big deal.

So what do you, as a type one, need to keep in mind when it comes to creativity?

It will be tempting to turn this into a burden. It can be very easy for type ones to pick a creative outlet that requires a lot of perfecting. I encourage you to hold your creativity lightly. I'm not saying that you shouldn't do something meticulous—many ones enjoy that process— just be willing to walk away when it quits feeling fun and starts to feel burdensome.

- Set a deadline for when you're done. It can be tempting to keep refining and refining. Set a time limit on your editing process and be happy with where you leave it.

- Speak kind words over what you've made at the end of every creative session. I like to think of this as treating your creation like another person. Don't look at it and say, "You'd be so much better if you just . . ." or "Ugh, I hate you." Look for the good in what you make and be proud of yourself for giving it time and attention.
- Share it with someone who appreciates beautiful things. Don't share it with your most critical friend or someone who doesn't "get it," share it with someone who loves to enjoy things. Let them share their inner voice with you for a minute. This will help you re-wire your own inner critic and positively incentivize you to keep creating.
- Think of the last time you had a creative impulse. Maybe it was a warmth in your belly or a rising in your chest or a feeling like you just wanted to do something, but you shoved it down and silenced the desire. Maybe it was dancing or writing or finger painting. Think to the last time you felt creatively excited, and follow that feeling. This is a safe space for you to get in touch with your impulses and play with what it feels like to just let yourself have what you want in a nourishing and supportive way.
- Pick a small corner of your house and get it exactly how you'd like it. This can be a really great way to expend some of that perfecting energy—put it into a single small project that you can enjoy for days and weeks to come.
- Get really into rough drafts. Have fun with doing a rough version of your creative outlet. You can always go back and refine. There's no reason for it to be perfect right out of the gate. Play with getting it out of you as quickly as possible. See how it feels just to create without refining in the initial creation phase.

Dear One

I hope you know you're good. I hope you know that by simply holding the awareness of who you want to be in the world, you are becoming that person. I hope that you leave this chapter knowing that you are just right exactly as you are. That waking up every day and putting in the effort to exist with the integrity that you do is more than anyone expects of you.

You are good.

Just as you are.

You are good.

Life is unpredictable and it can be tempting to try and make it all make sense. It's tempting to flirt with the idea that we can make the world exactly what feels right to us.

I know that you are hard on yourself, and I know that the work can seem never-ending, and I'm certain that at times you feel tired.

Let this page be a place for you to rest.

Right here in this moment, there is nothing expected of you. You are enough.

You are perfect.

No more effort.
No more striving.
You are good.
Exactly as you are.

GIVER

LOVER

HELPER

HIDDEN WARRIOR

Type Two

*"I often believe that I am as worthy as I am lovable,
that my worth is related to how wanted I am."*

"Let me do that for you."	Helps people move	Finishes 1000 projects for other people before starting their own	Store Manager.	"Yes."
Remembers the tiny things people tell them about themselves	Takes care of the dishes	Has people over for dinner	Cooking and cleaning are literal joys.	Always gives better gifts than they receive
"I shouldn't have to tell you how to love me . . ."	Hears the life stories of strangers	2	"Bless their heart."	Can literally read minds
"Honestly, I don't need anything."	How many texts are too many texts to send in a row?	"All I need is a 'thank you.'"	Dessert.	"Hey, are we good?"
Anticipates the needs of others	"Would you like to meet in person?"	Drops by with food	Relationships are life.	"Are you thirsty?"

AT AN AMUSEMENT PARK

By Enneagram type.

1 - THE ONE WITH THE MAP.

2 - THE ONE WITH THE SNACKS.

3 - THE ONE WITH THE FAST PASS.

4 - THE ONE WITH THE CHILDHOOD MEMORIES.

5 - THE ONE WHO KNOWS WHICH RIDES ARE THE BEST AND WHEN THE LINES ARE SHORT.

6 - THE ONE WITH THE SUNSCREEN.

7 - THE ONE WHO RIDES THE SAME ROLLERCOASTER TEN TIMES IN A ROW.

8 - THE ONE WHO DOES EVERYTHING IN ONE DAY.

9 - THE ONLY ONE NOT STRESSED OUT.

@enneagramandcoffee

ABOUT TYPE TWO

Basic Desire: "It's important to me that I'm liked."

Basic Fear: "What if no one ever loves me as I am?"

Type twos are helpful, generous, warm, and loving. They learned somewhere along the way that love is earned through what we do for other people. They tend to see the world as a sea of emotional temperatures, picking up the energy that people are sharing and then adjusting their own behavior to meet the needs they perceive in the room. The impulse to serve, for a type two, isn't necessarily conscious. In fact, to most type twos it's second nature and seems like the most natural thing in the world to step in and meet the needs of someone—especially someone they don't know very well.

Type twos are considerate, patient, gracious, forgiving, and likely the person who has made you feel the most loved in your life.

I titled type twos the "Hidden Warrior" because, while they are kind and sometimes sweet, there is a fierce power inside them. It's not uncommon for type twos to feel underestimated in the sharing of their kindness. They are powerful in their service, and I believe that should be honored.

Most type twos spend a lot of their time and energy focused on the state of relationships in their life. While most of us value healthy relationships, type twos build their lives around relationships. They are always aware of where they stand with people and if they are as close as they would like to be with those in their life. The beautiful thing about being in relationships with type twos is that they often see us as we wish to be seen. They call out the good in us and allow us to share with them who we are, and they take our word for it.

I believe the hardest thing about being a type two is the moment he or she realizes that others aren't spending as much of their energy concerned with relationships as he or she is. It can be quite hard for type twos to have their love matched by others. This is fine, except that type twos often interpret this as a lack of caring for them, which can trigger their type pattern into believing that they are not loved and, therefore, are not worthy of love.

I think it's particularly important for type twos to recognize that others are orienting in the world with a different lens. They are not ignoring the type twos' feelings but aren't aware of them as their primary focus of attention. Type twos will always have to ask for help way more than the people in a relationship with them. That's where things get tricky for the type two, though. One of the unseen and uncomfortable truths about type twos is that their vice is pride—the belief that they are the only ones without need. When a type two understands that they have needs and won't push people away by asking for those needs to be met, a deep freedom can occur.

SUBTYPES OF TYPE TWO

The following subtypes of type two are based on the three instinctual variants and how those interact with how type twos attempt to get their needs met without asking. The self-preservation type two does this by being "cute" or childlike, the social type two tries to be powerful and influential, and the sexual type two uses flattery and seduction.

SELF-PRESERVATION

- Cute or childlike behavior
- Playful
- Wants to be loved just for existing
- Pleasure-seeking
- Often dependent on others
- More guarded than other type twos
- Wants to be close to people, but often pushes people away at the same time
- Can look like a type four or seven

SOCIAL

- Ambitious
- Influential
- Focused on serving environments
- Seeks to be close to those in power
- Serves others as a method to advance their career/status
- More aware of their public image
- Often a leader
- More introverted than other type twos
- Can look like a type three or eight

SEXUAL

- Seductive
- Flattering
- Has the hardest time letting go of love that isn't working
- Seeks a strong bond with someone who will meet his or her needs
- Focuses attention and seduction on particular individuals
- Sexy, irresistible, and charming
- Can look like a type three or four

TYPE TWO AND WINGS

As a type two, you can pull from either of your wings to help round out your personality. You may find that you already lean in one direction more than the other. However, you have access to the skills and vices of both wings. Here are some qualities you can borrow from your neighbors:

TYPE ONE WING

With this wing, you can pull in the purpose for your service and focus on self-improvement and service of the greater good. Pulling in the type one wing is often helpful in humanitarian work, being willing to do hard work so that the suffering of the world can be relieved.

TYPE THREE WING

With this wing, you can tap into your social side and pull in your ability and desire to host and entertain friends. Utilize the high side of type three when you have a goal you want to achieve or if you're at a networking event and want to make connections. When this wing is dominant, you may find that you feel more sociable, charming, and ambitious.

TYPE TWO AND LINES

When in stress, the type two moves to type eight, and when in rest, they move to type four. With that understanding, here's what you may want to keep in mind in your relationship to stress and self-care.

RECOGNIZING YOUR STRESS

When stressed out, type twos may find themselves becoming resentful or harsh like the average-to-low levels of type eight. They may be more blunt and direct with what they've been given and more demanding of appreciation for the role they play in the lives of the people they love.

SELF-CARE INFUSION

When you start to feel this way, you have the tools you need to care for yourself by using the high side of type four. Take time to acknowledge honestly how you are feeling. Spend time alone. Be intentional about meeting your own needs and being fully self-indulgent in regard to hearing and validating your own feelings and emotions. I recommend that type twos take this time to give themselves whatever it is they are wishing someone else would give them. If you need to hear "Thank you for helping me today," say to yourself, "Thank you for helping them today. I am so grateful for who you are." If you want them to take you out to a nice dinner—take yourself out to your favorite restaurant.

RECOGNIZING STAGNATION

In the same way that you can intentionally use the emotionally attuned elements of type four to relieve stress, you can also use it by accident. Type fours are often driven by their emotions and can easily focus solely on what is going wrong. As a type two, you may see yourself slipping into this behavior and focusing on what is missing or daydreaming about a different life, without creating one for yourself or asking directly for what you need.

MOTIVATION INFUSION

This is where it's helpful to bring in the high side of type eight. Allow yourself to be direct and honest about your needs well before you are resentful. Speak up about your boundaries and deal breakers at the beginning of a relationship instead of when they've been crossed hundreds of times. Fear less that you'll push people away by asking for what you need and communicating proactively what feels good to you in relationships (romantic or otherwise).

LEVELS OF HEALTH

HEALTHY
In their healthiest state, type twos are able to give without expectation because they've learned how to meet their own needs. They no longer hold guilt for taking care of themselves and, therefore, are able to be truly altruistic. They are joyous, gracious, and humble, and they give unconditional love to themselves and others.

AVERAGE
In most cases, our type twos are giving with an unconscious desire to receive something in return. They crave to be liked/loved in relationships and can become consumed with focusing on how others feel about them. They may find themselves possessive in relationships and overly worried about losing the people in their lives to someone else. They may feel taken advantage of and overextended and will hold that as their reason that the people in their lives must remain close to them.

UNHEALTHY
In their unhealthiest state, type twos may find themselves driving people away with their aggressive over-giving. They rationalize the reactions of others by believing they are selfish people who don't appreciate what the type two has done for them. It is not uncommon for type twos in this state to play the role of victim as an unconscious method of gaining sympathy and encouraging others to step in and take care of them.

GETTING H.O.N.E.S.T. FOR TYPE TWO

What I believe is pretty remarkable about type twos is their ability to deeply love. To show us all what it means to be truly human. You hold this incredible space for people to open up and share and be completely loved for exactly where they are in a given moment. What is heartbreaking for me is the thought that this space is so rarely held for you in return. I imagine that could be a very lonely feeling. I want to encourage you to enter this section with full permission to show up for yourself with the same force that you do for someone you love. After all, the relationship you have with yourself is the only one that will be with you from the moment you are born to the moment you exit this earth. You deserve for that to be the most loving of all.

HONOR YOUR STRENGTHS

The first step is to take time to get really honest with yourself about what makes you amazing. Celebrate all of the elements of your personality that you love. If it's tricky for you to think of things you love about yourself, consider what you do and who you are that contributes positively to the world around you.

A few things that are amazing about type twos:
- You are loving.
- You are kind.
- You are warm and welcoming.
- You are able to see the good in people that they aren't always able to see themselves.
- You are powerful beyond measure.
- You are generous.
- You are like a home in human form—a place of safety for those in need of rest.
- You are charming.

- You are empathetic.
- You are lovable just as you are.

It's important that you know the goal isn't to avoid being a type two. You don't need to reject everything that you are—even your strengths. It's simply about holding the awareness for what is keeping you away from your essence. It's OK that your good qualities are part of your type pattern—it doesn't make them less good.

Take some time to write out your personal strengths below.

_____

_____

_____

_____

_____

OPEN YOUR EYES TO BLIND SPOTS

A part of me hates to have this conversation with type twos. It's not that you can't handle it—you are one of the strongest types in the Enneagram. It's more that you've spent so much of your life focused on loving others well and neglecting your own needs, and here comes the Enneagram all like, "Hey, you aren't doing that for the reasons you think you are." It makes me feel like a jerk to share that with you.

However, the truth is that it's all happening at once. You are kind and lovely and good. At the same time, it's important that we acknowledge and get honest about your motivations so that when you share your kindness, it is clear to both you and the other person that you are doing it from a place of non-attachment. We have to trudge through this mud to get you to the other side and the freedom of being TRULY loved! Are you ready for freedom?

A few things to keep in mind as a type two:

1. You aren't giving just to give.
As children, type twos believed that they were not loved for who they were but instead had to earn it. The pattern started early for them to focus on the needs of others, often taking care of their parental figures as a way to receive the affection that they craved. This created a pattern of behavior for type twos that giving is a way to receive. What you are hoping to receive could be different depending on the circumstances. Sometimes it's simply to be liked, other times it's to be close to those who are in charge or to get a physical or emotional need met.

You have needs too.

This giving in order to receive is also a symptom of the belief that you are not allowed to have needs of your own, and if you do express those needs, you will push people away. With relationships being your primary focus, it can feel like death to ask for something. The last thing you want is to push people away. Therefore, when you have a need, you may find yourself giving as a way to get it met. You are lonely—so you buy someone dinner so they'll spend time with you. You want someone to write you a letter, so you write them a letter as a way of initiating that connection.

The tricky piece of this is that most of this is happening unconsciously, so you may not even realize that you are acting out of a place of need. Instead you may feel as though you are simply giving and giving, and for some reason you feel unappreciated. The work here is learning to assess what you need somewhere in between feeling the need and serving another.

2. Neglecting your needs is actually hurting your relationships.
Perhaps the most important thing that type twos can learn is that not asking for your needs to be met is the exact behavior that pushes away the people you are trying to keep close by not asking. I know it's a mind trip, right?

Here's what happens when you don't ask for what you need:
- You may become invasive in the lives of those you care about—meeting needs and giving unsolicited advice where it's not wanted.
- You may find yourself letting your resentment out sideways—becoming snappy or irritable and not the warm, loving person that you are in your essence.
- You may find yourself becoming highly emotional and inauthentic—expressing your sadness in intense ways that manipulate the people around you or attempting to repress your negative feelings and, therefore, not connecting with people in the honest way that they're used to.

All of this isn't who you are. This is who you are when you are neglecting yourself. That is why it is SO important for type twos to intentionally check in with what they need every single day and do everything in their power to make sure that they give it to themselves.

3. Your worth has nothing to do with how others see you.
So much of the lower levels of behavior in our type twos comes from a deep desire to know that they are worthy of love. To have someone look you in the eye and say, "You are loved, just for being exactly who you are." In the attempt to receive that feedback, you can find yourself committing all of these unhelpful behaviors and then realizing that receiving that love once isn't enough—you need it again and again

and again. There is no satisfying a need that we are trying to get met by someone else.

The work here is to find your worth and your love from inside yourself. We all know this, though, right? I can hear people now, "Self-love; I know, I know!" Yet how often do we put it into practice?

For the type two, diving deep into the world of self-love and unconditional self-acceptance will bring balm to the wounds you are trying to heal with the love of another. You have it inside of you already.

Type two energy tends to move up and out. Scanning the room for those in need of love and pouring it out on them from the depths of your soul. I want you to experience moving your energy throughout your own person. Check in with yourself and pour that same love, acceptance, and flattery right back into your soul.

4. Find healthy ways to express your emotions.
Finally, our type twos have a difficult time with their emotions. You may feel everything as intensely as a type four, but you may reject the negative emotions by repressing them and attempting not to give them a voice. Often, this happens out of a pursuit to be the kind of person people like/love and a belief that positive people are more enjoyed then those with negative emotions. The trouble is that your negative feelings still exist with or without your attention. In these moments, they are more likely to come out as an outburst, as manipulative behavior, or—for lack of a better term—as martyr syndrome.

Your emotions are worth their time in the spotlight. Allow them to exist as they are. Be OK with the act of being just as human as the rest of us. I recommend that type twos check in with their feelings each day and be honest about what is present in that moment. You may want to try asking yourself, "What is here for me today?" Either talk it out loud to yourself in the car (did you know that type twos are verbal processors?) or write it down in a journal.

NOTE YOUR SUPPORT PLAN

This is the part of the process where we get to talk about finding what actually serves YOU when it comes to creating a life that you love. This is fun for me to share with type twos because, so often, type twos focus on being the support plan for other people that they forget to create a support plan for themselves.

The primary work we are doing here is to help you acknowledge you have needs, feel loved and lovable within yourself, and ask for what you need from those in your life with healthy boundaries and love requests.

A few things that may support you in the process:
- Write yourself really indulgent love letters and then throw them away.
- Take yourself out on regular dates to the movies, nice restaurants, or art galleries—wherever you want to go.
- Set healthy boundaries at the first sign of resentment.
- Check in with your needs every single day.
- Give yourself the affirmations you are craving from other people.
- Take time to travel alone.
- Create a morning practice of asking yourself, "What's here for me today?"
- Take a season of "no"—set aside a series of days/weeks/months where your only work is in building the muscle of not overgiving. Turn down every opportunity to serve that comes your way. (See how loved you still are during this season, and part of you will be set free.)

- Carve out a few hours every week that are yours and yours alone. Turn off your phone (Everyone will be fine.) and just do whatever you want to do.
- Greet your urge to serve with curiosity, asking, "Am I in need of something in this moment?"
- Practice only giving when you expect absolutely NOTHING in return. Check in and ask, "Would I still want to do this if I knew they weren't going to even say 'thank you'?"

What can you do this week to get really honest with how you feel, ask for what you need, and love the pants off of yourself?

EXPLORE YOUR RELATIONSHIPS

So far, you've honored your strengths, gotten really honest with yourself about your blind spots, and set aside a plan of support in the process. Now it's time to talk about relationships. It's all well and good to do all of this work on our own, but what do we do when someone else disrupts our perfect synchronicity of self-compassion? This is where we get to explore what you bring into your relationships. What do you positively contribute? What do you do that doesn't help you be the warm, generous, loving, and accepting person that you are in your essence?

Beautiful things that type twos bring to their relationships:
- Acceptance of exactly who we are.
- Nourishment for our souls (and sometimes our bodies).
- Showing up when we need help.
- Seeing and valuing us for who we are.
- Generosity with your time, resources, and kind words.
- Making people feel comfortable and safe in your presence.
- Showing people what it means to be loved and to share love.
- Allowing us to be human with you.

A few things that may not be serving your relationships:

- Using "tactics" to get your needs met instead of asking directly.
- Believing that no one loves you in the way that you love them.
- Overburdening yourself with giving to others and then resenting that they aren't doing the same for you.
- Sharing inauthentic flattery as a way to win people over instead of showing up honestly when you are hurt.
- Prioritizing the affection of new people and people you have not yet "won over" instead of the people who are closest to you.
- Remaining possessive of those who you love out of fear that they will lose interest.

The reason we're talking about this—even if it's uncomfortable and sometimes painful—is because in the long run it will bring you so much relief. Holding the truth that both of these lists exist simultaneously is the key to ease in your relationships. Knowing what you can control and what isn't yours to worry about can be an extremely relaxing move to make. That tiny list up there, that's it. Think about that. You are doing so much right!

Take a few minutes to think of your own lists. Write down what you personally bring to your relationships, both positively and negatively.

Now, take a few moments to think of the three most important relationships in your life. Write out how you would like for them to feel. How would they change if you could imagine a world where they were exactly as you hoped? What about your lists would need to shift in order to have the relationships that you want?

SOFTEN YOUR PATH

OK, so we've established what makes you amazing. (Way to go, by the way!) We've covered what areas of your life may be in need of some tender love and care. We've even discussed how to support yourself in this growth. Let's now talk about how we're going to keep this process going even when other people's needs start to arise. Because I know you'll be tempted to push yourself aside and de-prioritize this work . . .

I want to give you these four soft internal shifts to make. Just four things to hold on to each and every day that will help you in the work of being your healthiest type two self.

1. Check in with your needs every day.

I almost titled this "Know your motivations," but as I started typing the paragraph, I realized that without knowing your needs, it's impossible to know your motivations. Most type twos are in a constant state of awareness of how others want to feel. (So cool, btw.) Because of this, it can be hard to sift through which actions are manipulative in nature and which are genuine acts of selfless giving. In order to do that, you HAVE to know what you need and be able to meet those needs yourself.

Check in with yourself each and every morning. Ask yourself what you need and do your best to meet that need before offering your help to anyone!

2. Flatter yourself daily.

I mean this. Flirt with yourself like it is your job. Walk by the mirror and check yourself out. Write yourself letters and tell yourself how awesome you are. Dote all over yourself and bask in your own magnificent type two luminance.

3. Prioritize authenticity.

In everything you say and do, I encourage you to run it through the filter of, "Is this the most honest action for me to take?" Make radical authenticity a top priority for yourself. Are you feeling terrible today? Be honest about it. Are you missing a friend? Text them and let them know you're thinking of them. Are you wanting to be taken on a nice date?

4. Ask directly for what you want.
Watch how much easier it is to give and receive love when you are being one hundred percent open and honest about who you are, what you need, and how you feel.

TURN THAT INTO SOMETHING BEAUTIFUL

Creativity is important for all types. It's important that you take the time to see how you feel and what you have to express and develop a hobby that is only for you and serves no one else (well, at least not in the immediate sense of the word).

So, what do you, as a type two, need to keep in mind when it comes to creativity?

- It will be the easiest thing in the world to de-prioritize this step and give your time away to people and things that need your attention rather than giving it to yourself. You will have to make this a priority.
- You will be tempted to bring someone else into this process. I encourage you to make this your own thing. Take time each week to be alone and make something beautiful.
- Don't share it with anyone for a little while. Just create without feedback.
- There is no reason for this to be the same thing every week. You can pick up a single hobby and just do it all the time. However, if you find that you're losing interest or you're de-prioritizing it, try switching it up and doing something new.

- You may have an easier time doing something tactile. A lot of type twos find themselves resentful of time behind a computer. Try creative outlets like painting, knitting, gardening, or anything else that you can do with your hands.

~~~~~~~~

Dear Two

You are so worthy of love just as you are. Not only were you born with intrinsic value, you have grown into someone whose sole focus is to make others feel seen, heard, and accepted. That's so beautiful.

It's important for you to know that you aren't at risk of becoming a selfish monster. I know it scares you to think of taking all of this time for yourself, asking for your needs to be met, setting healthy boundaries, etc.

I know that it's triggering all of the parts of you that fear pushing people away. I want you to know that the only people you can push away by asking for what you need are those who are prioritizing their needs over yours anyway. You will only be losing those who are in no way giving you the same place in their hearts that you do in yours.

Here's the really big thing I want you to digest: just because someone chooses not to remain close to you does not in any way mean that you are not worthy of being close to.

It is likely that, most of your life, you have built the dynamic that you are there to serve and others are there to receive. With that pattern comes some people who are VERY comfortable in the receiving mode and less comfortable in the giving. Let those people float away. They aren't your people.

Your people are the ones who have been waiting your entire friend-ship for you to say the sweet, healthy, and magical words, "I'm feeling a little _____. Do you mind if we _____?"

You can do this.
You are worthy of this.
You are so freaking loved!
Just as you are and not for what you do.

ACHIEVER

MOTIVATOR

PERFORMER

EMPOWERING
MOTIVATOR

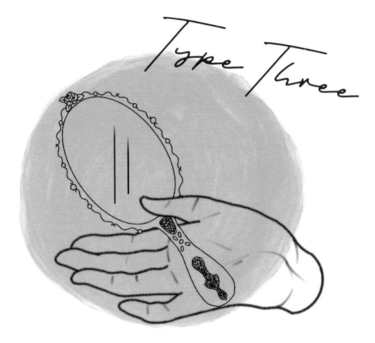

Type Three

*"I believe I will be OK as long as I am constantly
achieving new things."*

BINGO

"I've got this."	Great at first impressions.	Magical ability to read a room.	I love my job.	Not afraid to invest in their future.
Healthy competition.	"You are the sum of the five people you surround yourself with."	Multi-tasking.	Trendy AF.	Goes hard and then crashes
"Don't speak to me while I'm working."	"What do you mean 'take weekends off'?"	3	Imposter Syndrome.	Goal-setting.
Teacher's pet.	Progress over perfection.	Sales numbers.	"But, I love to work!"	Works on vacation
Designer items.	"Figure it out!"	Morning routines.	Podcasts on your commute.	"No excuses."

CELEBRATIONS

By Enneagram type.

1 - "LET ME JUST FINISH UP THIS ONE THING FIRST . . ."

2 - "DON'T MAKE A FUSS OVER ME."

3 - "WHEN I HIT _ _ _ _ GOAL THEN I'M GOING TO REALLY CELEBRATE."
HITS GOAL "WHEN I HIT _ _ _ _ GOAL THEN I'LL CELEBRATE."

4 - "THERE'S A CELEBRATION IN EVERY LEAF, IN EVERY ROCK, IN EVERY
HEARTBEAT."

5 - "I CELEBRATE. IT'S JUST WITH A GOOD SCOTCH AND A GREAT
BOOK."

6 - "DON'T FLAKE ON ME, WE'RE GOING OUT TONIGHT!"

7 - "I FINISHED MY TAXES! WE SHOULD CELEBRATE!" *5 MIN. LATER* "I
GOT ALL OF MY WORK DONE FOR THE DAY! WE SHOULD CELEBRATE!"
A LITTLE BIT LATER "I FINISHED THE BOOK I WAS READING! WE SHOULD
CELEBRATE!"

8 - "I WENT AHEAD AND PLANNED OUR CELEBRATION. IT'S HAPPENING
ON FRIDAY SO WE'RE GOING TO HAVE TO WORK OVERTIME TO FINISH
BY THEN."

9 - "WHATEVER YOU WANT TO DO IS FINE! I DEFINITELY WANT TO DO
SOMETHING TO CELEBRATE...I'LL JUST BE HAPPY WITH WHATEVER."

@enneagramandcoffee

ABOUT TYPE THREE

Basic Desire: "It's important to me that I am accepted and viewed as worthwhile."

Basic Fear: "What if I'm only as worthy as what I can achieve?"

Type threes are driven, motivated, and goal-oriented. They learned somewhere along the way that their worth is determined by what they can achieve. They tend to orient in the world with an awareness of where they stand in comparison to other people and focus on always doing better, achieving more, and being generally enjoyed by others. Type threes are skilled at engaging with others. They can read body language, take the temperature of a room, and get a general feeling for how they can show up to be both liked and impressive. Type threes have very high standards for themselves and what they must accomplish, although it is often not their own ideals that drive this. Many type threes adopt their desires from society, their immediate family, or even their close friends. The focus becomes less on their personal agenda, and more on what is viewed as the most successful thing to be, based off the culture they are most entrenched in.

Type threes are inspiring, accomplished, capable, productive, efficient, and likely the person who makes you want to do more, be more, and dream bigger.

I titled type threes the "Empowering Motivators" because, in their essence, they serve as beautiful examples of what we are all capable of. They spend their lives in constant pursuit of excellence and, when at their best, encourage, motivate, and support us all in doing the same.

Most type threes spend a lot of their time and energy focused on the pursuit of their goals and the next level of success. While we all have an element of ourselves that would like to be successful, type threes feel as if they "need" to succeed in order not to be worthless. Because of this, the focus of attention for our type threes is almost exclusively on ensuring they do not waste away in the world remaining nameless.

I believe the hardest thing about being a type three is the reality that there is never an end point to all of this striving. Every level of success only reveals a new level to work toward. When this is your standard of self-worth, you find yourself on a constant race to the top. Eventually, for a lot of type threes, there's a realization that there is no actual "top." At this point, they wake up to the reality that success is in how you feel about your life, and that it's time to start enjoying life where they are now. The tricky thing with this is that in their pursuit of goals and success, they forgot to get to know themselves along the way. It can take type threes some time to figure out what actually does make them happy. They will need to enter into a season of reflection and self-curiosity that can be a bit disorienting for such an action-oriented type.

SUBTYPES OF TYPE THREE

The following subtypes of type three are based on the three instinctual variants and how they interact with the type three's relationship to achieving a successful image. The self-preservation type three focuses on success by working hard and doing the best job he or she can do; the social type three focuses on the recognition he or she can receive through success; the sexual type three is more focused on the success of being attractive to a potential partner and supporting successful people in their pursuits.

SELF-PRESERVATION
- Autonomous and self-sufficient

- Focused on being the best
- Goes beyond the appearance of being successful and truly works hard to be great at everything they do
- Rejects the desire to be noticed for achievements even though the desire is still present
- Work-focused
- Security-oriented
- Can look like a type one or six

SOCIAL

- The most able to make others feel comfortable around them
- Focused on higher and higher levels of success
- Most competitive of the subtypes
- Focused on relationships that will help achieve their goals
- Feel confident leading a group and can become impatient with ineffective leadership
- Struggles with impostor syndrome

SEXUAL

- Focused on finding the perfect love or being the perfect lover
- Enthusiastic supporter of the success of others
- Less driven with achieving goals, other than being attractive
- People-pleasing
- Can look like a type two or seven

TYPE THREE AND WINGS

As a type three, you can pull from either of your wings to help round out your personality. You may find that you already lean in one direction more than the other. However, you have access to the skills and vices of both wings. Here are some qualities you can borrow from your neighbors:

TYPE TWO WING

When pulling in this wing, you may find yourself feeling more sponta-neous. You may be more able to assess your emotions. Use this wing to utilize empathy and emotional awareness to prioritize your relation-ships. This wing can be strengthened when you need help communi-cating with loved ones and creating healthy, thriving relationships.

TYPE FOUR WING

With this wing, you can tap into your drive for perfecting and sharing your "craft." You may become more work-oriented and more focused on what you want to achieve in terms of your career or creative expression. You may find yourself more serious and task-oriented in the style of a type one. This wing can be strengthened when you need to figure out what you want, who you are, and what would make you truly happy.

TYPE THREE AND LINES

When in stress, the type three moves to type nine, and when in rest, they move to type six. With that understanding, here's what you may want to keep in mind in your relationship to stress and self-care:

RECOGNIZING YOUR STRESS

When stressed out, type threes may find themselves "numbing out," retreating to their couch and finding comfort in being home. They may end up cutting corners, ignoring their responsibilities, and essentially checking out from all of their hard work. Another side of this move for type threes that is a bit more long-term is the tendency to numb out on their own desires and accidentally remaining in careers, relationships, and roles that are of very little interest to them. They may do the bare minimum to remain in that environment with little or no zeal for what they're doing.

SELF-CARE INFUSION

When you start to feel this way, you have the tools you need to care for yourself. Using the high side of type six, you can prepare for these times in advance by either moderating your energy so that you are overworking much less and, therefore, not burning yourself out, or by preparing your work in advance when the energy is there and allowing for rest time when needed. You may also find that leaning into the team spirit of a type six will help ease the competitive nature that can keep you burning the candle at both ends. Adopting the philosophy that someone else's success does not take away from your own can be very therapeutic for type threes.

RECOGNIZING STAGNATION

In the same way that you can use the preparation and team-building elements of type six to relieve stress, you can also use it by accident. Type sixes tend to keep themselves very busy as a way to prove themselves to a particular organization or person. They value playing an intricate role in their community. This can further emphasize your desire to be seen in a certain light and even perpetuate your tendency to become who you need to be in order to achieve perceived success. You may also find yourself uncharacteristically anxious about your future and security.

MOTIVATION INFUSION

This is where it's helpful to bring in the high side of type nine. Bringing regular rest and stress-reducing activities into your life will help you maintain consistency, balance, and, ultimately, self-awareness. Remaining removed from conflict and "drama" will allow you the space to be less competitive and comparing so that you can remain present, available, and supportive of your peers.

LEVELS OF HEALTH

HEALTHY

In their healthiest state, type threes are able to integrate their desire to appear successful into the practice of becoming truly great at what they do. They release the belief that their worth is related to the way they are perceived and are able to focus on what would make them truly happy. This pursuit of their own happiness and self-acceptance allows them to finally feel truly successful.

AVERAGE

In most cases, our type threes are living with the fear that they will be outshined by others and, therefore, must stay in constant pursuit of more and better in order to stay relevant. At this level, it can be easy for a type three to get caught up in being self-promoting and "braggy," and he or she may amplify achievements in an attempt to stand out above the crowd.

UNHEALTHY

When angry, sad, defensive, or going through a long season without self-care, type threes may find themselves more and more afraid that they are without true worth and may convince themselves of false ideas of what they've achieved. They can become deceitful in their attempt to be impressive. They may become obsessively competitive with imagined competitors looking for any opportunity to make them seem less qualified or worthy of success.

GETTING H.O.N.E.S.T. FOR TYPE THREE

What I believe is pretty remarkable about type threes is the way you have this innate drive to keep showing up. You are relentless in the pursuit of living the life you want to live and fully capable of handling anything that life sends your way. You rarely back down from a challenge, pay attention to what has worked for others, and figure out how to market what works for you as well. What is equally heartbreaking for me is the thought that this remarkable force of energy can so easily be misdirected to building a persona that you are proud of without building in the depth that will bring you the true fulfillment that you're craving. For type threes, there's this underlying fear that you are in fact worthless. That can cause you to take on all kinds of forms and measures and push yourself past human capacity to prove that it isn't true. What I hope this section offers you is the space to find that worth without all of the extra effort and to hold celebration for just being a person in this world.

HONOR YOUR STRENGTHS

The first step is to take time to get really honest with yourself about what makes you amazing. Celebrate all of the elements of a personality that you love. If it's tricky for you to think of things you love about yourself, consider what you do and who you are that contributes positively to the world around you.

A few things that are amazing about type threes:
- You are capable of anything you set your mind to.
- You are adaptive.
- You are charming.
- You are in constant pursuit of growth.
- You are aware and engaged.
- You are likely very good at what you do.
- You are inspiring.

- You are not quick to back down from a challenge.
- You are a self-starter.
- You are innately worthy.

It's important that you know the goal isn't to avoid being a type three. You don't need to reject everything that you are—even your strengths. It's simply about holding the awareness for what is keeping you away from your essence. It's OK that your good qualities are part of your type pattern—it doesn't make them less good.

Take some time to write out your personal strengths below.

_____

_____

_____

_____

_____

OPEN YOUR EYES TO BLIND SPOTS

This is the point where we get to have what one of my favorite type threes calls #realtalk. I'm going to hand it to you very straight here because I know that you'll appreciate it. These right down here, these are the REAL things holding you back from finding the fulfillment that you are seeking. You are so capable of taking this by the horns and really making magic happen here, and by doing so, I know you will inspire so many others to live rich, fulfilled, and empowered lives.

A few things to keep in mind as a type three:

1. Other people aren't either your competition or your pathway to success.
As children, type threes learned that the path to approval was through their accomplishments. In that process, some part of their brains

absorbed the idea that if others are "better" than they are, they will not receive the approval that they crave. This can create a deprivation mindset around worthiness and the belief that there is only so much to go around. If someone around you is more "successful," then you think they must be absorbing all of the worth. The sooner you are able to see the reality that we are each worthy and unique in our own right, the sooner you will be able to find ease in the quietness of your mind.

In the same way, other people are also not simply tools for achieving more success. It can become easy to view others through the lens of what they can do for you. If they can pave a new path to success, you are more naturally inclined to align yourself with them. It's important to view people individually, hold space for who they really are, and value individuals for who they are, not just what they can do for you. This will result in deep relationships where you are able to be honest about all elements of yourself, not just the impressive ones. This is where the magic of life lives.

2. There is no destination.
The feeling that there is always a new peak to climb will leave you climbing mountain after mountain of success, reaching the top only to find a new peak in the distance. When we commit our lives to the constant pursuit of success, we deprive ourselves of the joy of truly living. The trouble is that striving for next, better, and more will never end, and you'll end up thirty to forty years down the road with a wall of gold medals but a depleted soul.

It's time to pause, look at your life, and ask yourself if you feel good living it. What do you want your life to look and feel like outside of what you want to achieve? Set your goals based on how you want to feel, so you can be clear that you are setting the goals you actually want.

How many famous people have to commit suicide before we learn that success doesn't equal happiness? Start thinking of success as how you feel in your day-to-day life and you will build the life you want to live.

3. Being appreciated for your achievements is like eating too much ice cream.

I imagine we all know the feeling of eating a giant bowl of ice cream. We get it in our heads that we can't wait to eat some ice cream. It sounds delicious and like exactly what we need, so we do what we need to do to get our bowl of ice cream. We enjoy it, but not quite as much as we thought we would. Once we finish, our stomach immediately hurts and we are uncomfortable. Then we wake up the next morning, and it's like the ice cream never happened and we are hungry again.

Living a life relying on the acknowledgments of what you've accomplished is the exact same thing. They seem like what you want. But when you get them, it feels good only for a moment, and at what cost to your mental and physical well-being? Not to mention, when they're gone, it leaves you in constant hunger for more.

It's important that you don't seek the praise from your accomplishments. Instead, focus on the way you want to feel from receiving the praise and create goals that help you feel the good feeling. (Psst—the feeling is the accomplishment.)

4. Failure is inevitable.

Most type threes spend what likely adds up to years of their life focused on dodging failure, either avoiding it altogether or attempting to hide it under fancy presentations of what pieces went right.

Failure is part of the process. The happiest and healthiest type threes I know have fully integrated failure into their lives. They celebrate their failures, they anticipate failure, and they don't assume that failing at something makes them a failure as a person.

This can be a hard lesson to learn and, unfortunately, is usually on the other side of multiple failures. However, it may be one of the most life-changing lessons for us all.

5. You can't outwork your feelings.

It's not uncommon for type threes to overwork, overschedule, and remain very busy as a way to avoid dealing with their deeper emotions. You can take on as many new projects, promotions, and tasks as you would like, but your feelings will be there waiting for you at the end of the day. In fact, ignored feelings do what things do best in the dark—they get scarier.

The more we ignore how we feel, the more the quiet times alone at home become dark and scary places to be. You are worthy of your attention. You are worthy of taking the time to sit with what's going on with you.

Some type threes have feelings that have been lurking in the shadows for years, even decades, quietly festering and making life feel lonelier than it has to be.

Carve out regular space to be honest with yourself about what is hard for you and what you're trying to ignore, and make sure that you have at least one person who you are one hundred percent vulnerable with about the hardest parts of life. This is non-negotiable, my friend. You are not only worthy of this time and attention, but also need it to be the truest version of yourself in the world.

NOTE YOUR SUPPORT PLAN

This is the part of the process where we get to talk about finding what actually serves you when it comes to creating a life that you love. This is cool for type threes because you've likely tried a lot of different self-growth methods in the past. You're not afraid of self-improvement.

The primary work we are doing here is in helping you to find space for yourself to be honest about what you really want, safety to be honest with the world about who you truly are, a balance of rest and work, and a ticket off of the hamster wheel of seeking constant validation for your achievements.

A few things that may support you in the process:

- Determine how you want to feel over the course of the next six months. Set goals that will help you experience that feeling.
- Establish at least one relationship in your life in which you are committed to being one hundred percent authentic about everything that is up for you at the moment.
- Notice when you are ignoring your physical and mental well-being in favor of achievement. Ask yourself what adjustment you can make each day to be more in tune with how you feel.
- Create a ritual for yourself to be honest about how you actually feel each day. Whether that's a journal entry, quick check-in, or meditation, make it anything that will allow you to sit for just a few moments with the truth of what is up with you.
- Do good work in secret. Refine your skills, add depth to what you're doing, make something you're proud of, and tell no one.
- Nothing can replace the muscle of appreciating your own hard work.
- Do something that embarrasses you regularly. Sing karaoke, act silly at the grocery store, or make a terrible face and take

a picture of it. Feel the freedom of releasing the need to appear to other people as someone to be admired.

- Let yourself sit with negative feedback without holding any more weight to it. We all fall short. You aren't any more of a failure because you are receiving feedback from someone.
- Practice asking yourself, "Why do I like this thing?" Is it because you really enjoy it, or is it because it's valued by people you want to admire you? Practice building the muscle of knowing what you want in the small things, like meals, places, and things.

What can you do this week to get really honest with how you feel, deepen your skills, and practice balance in your achievements?

EXPLORE YOUR RELATIONSHIPS

So far, you've honored your strengths, gotten really honest with yourself about your blind spots, and set aside a plan of support in the process. Now it's time to talk about relationships. It's all well and good to do all of this work on our own but what do we do when someone else disrupts our perfect synchronicity of self-compassion? This is where we get to explore what you bring into your relationships. What do you positively contribute? What do you do that doesn't serve your work of being the warm, generous, loving, and accepting person that you are in your essence?

Beautiful things that type threes bring to their relationships:
- Showing us what is possible for us.
- Helping us succeed in our own pursuits.
- Pushing us to do more than we think we're capable of.
- Often taking on the role of provider.
- You're inspiring, engaging, and charming.
- Knowing how to show up for people in the ways they need.

- Remaining warm, inviting, and interesting when meeting friends of friends or friends of your significant other.
- Staying on the path of self-improvement, working to the best that you can be.

A few things that may not be serving your relationships:
- Placing tasks above people and often forgetting to take time for people you care about.
- Believing that negative feedback means that you've failed and, therefore, struggling to accept and integrate difficult feedback.
- Pushing people before they're ready or in directions they may not be wanting to go.
- Pursuing relationships with people who can further your success and releasing those that you feel "hold you back."
- Hiding the truth of who you are, what you've actually achieved, and what you've done as a way to remain impressive to those you engage with.
- Crafting a persona that you are proud of without doing the deeper work of being who you want to be. (This can leave you feeling as though people love the persona of who you are but no one knows the real you.)

The reason we're talking about this—even if it's uncomfortable and sometimes painful—is because in the long run it will bring you so much relief. Holding the truth that both of these lists exist simultaneously is the key to ease in your relationships. Knowing what you can control and what isn't yours to worry about can be an extremely relaxing move to make. That tiny list up there, that's it. Think about that. You are doing so much right!

Take a few minutes to think of your own lists. Write down what you personally bring to your relationships, both positively and negatively.

Now, take a few moments here to think of the three most important relationships in your life. Write out how you would like for them to feel. How would they change if you could imagine a world where they were exactly as you hoped? What about your lists would need to shift in order to have the relationships that you want?

SOFTEN YOUR PATH

OK, so we've established what makes you amazing. (Way to go, by the way!) We've covered what areas of your life may be in need of some tender love and care. We've even discussed how to support yourself in this growth. Let's now talk about how we're going to keep this process going even when work, life, and tasks start flooding in, because I know you'll be tempted to put your tasks above what you need!

I want to give you these three soft internal shifts to make—just three things to hold on to each and every day that will help you in the work of being your healthiest type three self.

1. Practice radical honesty.

So many type three struggles can be healed through this one act alone. The act of deceiving others about your credentials and state of mind is a self-perpetuating cycle. You worry that you are only as worthy as your achievements, but you talk only about achievements so you only receive praise for your achievements. When these achievements are amplified or made up, then you are even more made to feel that no one would love the real you. Stop it! We want to love you. Truly. The people in your life aren't there because of some weird award or some figure in the bank. They're there because they think you're interesting. Let them get to know the real you. This is the only way for you to have true meaningful relationships in your life.

2. Check in on those emotions.

Remember earlier when we spoke about those shadowy little buggers that hide out in the dark and get scarier and scarier until you either deal with them or they start to infiltrate your life in not-so-pretty ways? Yeah, those guys. Go ahead and catch them before they start to get shadowy. Take time every day to be fully present with yourself. Are you sad? Feel it! Are you angry? Acknowledge it! Are you scared? What of and why?

Dealing with them right away will help them not to become little monsters under your bed that grow bigger and bigger until they eat you alive. They just want to be heard. Talk to them.

3. Keep some things to yourself.

So much of the type three's life has been hiding things that should be shared and sharing things that aren't as important. While it's important for you to share your honest emotions, the truth of who you are, and what you really want—it may be just as important for you to do some things that you're proud of without telling anyone.

Get really good at guitar or learn a new skill at your job, and keep it to yourself. It's totally possible for you to find a place of delight in knowing that you have accomplished something, and you aren't waiting for someone to notice it.

Of course, the muscle memory of waiting is going to be there. Notice it, say "Hi," and tell yourself, "I'm proud of you." And move on with your day.

TURN THAT INTO SOMETHING BEAUTIFUL

Creativity is important for all types. It's important that you take the time to see how you feel, what you have to express, and develop a hobby that is only for you and serves no one else (well, at least not in the immediate sense of the word).

So what do you, as a type three, need to keep in mind when it comes to creativity?

- You will likely have to carve out intentional time to make this happen. We both know your schedule isn't light. Trust me when I say it's worth it.
- If you can bring an element of playfulness into your creation, it will be really rewarding. Explore what it feels like to just let go and see what feels good!
- Don't monetize your creative expression—at least, not right now. Give it at least six months to a year before you even entertain the idea of making it into a business. Let it be pure expression for a while.
- Ask yourself what you "feel" like making and let that lead the way. Play with this practice in creative outlets so that you can be more equipped to integrate it into the bigger areas of life.

Dear Three

I hope you know that you are worthy. Just as you are.

You are incredible.

Each and every fiber of your being is innately deserving of your utmost adoration.

There is no amount of money, success, or beauty that will make you more or less worthy. Your worth was determined at birth and remains constant throughout your life.

The access you have to believing that and truly digesting it is found on the other side of honest connection with both yourself and others.

Open up your heart to those close to you and feel the rich satisfaction of being accepted for exactly who you are. I promise you won't ever want to go back.

Oh yeah, and did I mention that you aren't an impostor? You deserve your success and will continue to deserve good things in your life.

No one is waiting to "find you out," and you are safe to enjoy the fruits of all that hard labor.

It's time for you to rest, experience safety, and get to know exactly who you are!

I'm rooting for you.

ARTIST

ROMANTIC

INDIVIDUALIST

MEANING MAKER

Type Four

"It's the most important thing for me to always be true to who I am."

BINGO

"Did you see that beautiful tree?"	Classical music.	Murikami.	"I'm a . . ."	Hates Pier One Imports
Fairly certain that you're going to die young.	Looks out the window while crying	Pretends their life is a movie	Black sheep.	Sad movies.
"No one gets me."	Loves being the rarest type on the Enneagram	4	"But that's been done before . . ."	Gets into archery, buys all the supplies, never does archery
Kind of likes going through breakups	"Come here. Go away. Don't leave."	Cries while telling a story	"Maybe I'll just never be a . . ."	Romanticizes tradition
"That smell reminds me of childhood."	Has a very specific aesthetic	"If I could only _____, then I'd be able to _____."	"I just feel like I don't have something that everyone else has."	"You just need to tell people how you feel."

GROCERY STORE HABITS

By Enneagram type.

1 - ALWAYS PUTS THEIR CART BACK IN THE RIGHT PLACE.

2 - "YOU NEED ANYTHING FROM THE STORE?"

3 - LISTENS TO PODCASTS WHILE SHOPPING.

4 - SHOPS AT WHOLE FOODS.

5 - KNOWS WHICH STORE HAS THE RIGHT THINGS AND ONLY SHOPS THERE.

6 - DOUBLE-CHECKS THE WEIGHT OF PRE-PACKAGED PRODUCE.

7 - BUYS THEMSELVES A TREAT.

8 - IN AND OUT.

9 - CONSISTENTLY BUYS THE SAME TRUSTY ITEMS.

@enneagramandcoffee

ABOUT TYPE FOUR

Basic Desire: "It's important to me that I find an identity that expresses the truth of who I am and helps me find my significance."

Basic Fear: "What if I am not significant in any way?"

Type fours are deep, expressive, and nostalgic. They often felt rejected by or different from their family of origin. This created a deep desire in type fours not only to be understood but also to find their personal significance. Type fours tend to orient in the world with an awareness of what is missing. They see themselves as fundamentally flawed and often turn that internal experience into an external representation of being different or unique. Type fours walk through the world with the belief that there is something that everyone else seems to have but that they don't possess. The target for this may change from gumption to work ethic to charisma to anything else under the sun. Through this belief, they may find themselves feeling easily defeated. There can be a "Why try if I'm only going to mess it up anyway?" approach to things.

Type fours are emotionally in tune, aesthetically gifted, authentic, romantic, and idealistic, and have a beautiful ability to see the world as living art.

I titled type fours the "Meaning Makers" because, in their essence, I believe we need type fours to show us the beauty in human experience. They demand depth, create richness, and don't shy away from the human condition. We are all more able to feel, express, and experience the world in its complexity because we have type fours in our atmosphere.

Most type fours spend a lot of their time and energy focused on what they are missing and how they are falling short. While we all have the tendency to see ourselves as "less than," type fours develop their worldview from the perspective that they are fatally flawed and, therefore, different from everyone else—not only different but also somehow inferior. Because of this, a significant amount of energy goes into finding something that defines them, something they can identify with as their "thing," something outside of themselves to begin to craft their significance.

I believe the hardest thing about being a type four is the idea that there will be something outside of themselves that will help them create their importance while, at the same time, having a hunch at their innate greatness. What I mean by this is that many type fours see the world in terms of what they are missing, yet inside of themselves feel very special, intelligent, and deep. They know that they will be great at something if they can just find what that something is. This can lead the type four to pick up new things and give them up when they aren't immediately gifted at them. They daydream of someone walking up to them and saying, "You look like you'd make an amazing cello player. Here's the best cello in the world; now play!"—and it all falling together.

It takes time and patience for type fours to wake up to the reality that anyone who has ever been great has had to learn and fail and learn again. While that may be easy for many type fours to say to another person, there's a sneaking suspicion when they fail that they may actually be as terrible at life as they think they are, thus repeating the cycle.

A lot of the work for our type fours comes down to realizing that they are not any more or less human than everyone else and that's just perfect.

SUBTYPES OF TYPE FOUR

The following subtypes of type four are based on the three instinctual variants and how those interact with the type four's relationship to suffering. The self-preservation type four focuses on enduring suffering, the social type four focuses on how much they are suffering, and the sexual type four focuses on making others suffer because they have suffered before.

SELF-PRESERVATION
- Learns to live in pain, holding pride for themselves for how much suffering they can endure
- Works hard to get what others have that they feel they are lacking
- Often a humanitarian
- Craves the struggle and may find ways to place themselves in the path of struggle
- Values resilience
- Can look like a type one or three

SOCIAL
- The most sensitive of the subtypes
- Craves recognition and understanding through their suffering
- More likely to depend on others for help
- Has a heightened focus on their emotions
- Feels guilty for wanting things
- Often relates to the feeling of being a "misfit"
- Often feels like a victim
- Quick to help others but won't take care of their own needs
- Compares themselves to others and believes that they are "less than"
- Can look like a type six

SEXUAL

- The most competitive of the subtypes
- Believes that they have suffered so much that they should make others suffer
- Angry
- Assertive
- Demanding
- Craves intensity of emotion
- Holds a combination of feeling inferior while also craving to feel superior
- Can look like a type eight

TYPE FOUR AND WINGS

As a type four, you can pull from either of your wings to help round out your personality. You may find that you already lean in one direction more than the other. However, you have access to the skills and vices of both wings. Here are some qualities you can borrow from your neighbors:

TYPE THREE WING

When pulling in this wing, you may find yourself tapping into the ambitious side of your creativity—turning your ideas into plans and potentially even making money from your art. You allow yourself to be more success-oriented and driven and create platforms for yourself to be heard in your authenticity.

TYPE FIVE WING

With this wing, you can pair your introspection with perception and tap into intense and creative thought. You may find yourself able to dive deep into the process of creating just for the sake of making something beautiful.

TYPE FOUR AND LINES

When in stress, the type four moves to type two, and when in rest, they move to type one. With that understanding, here's what you may want to keep in mind in your relationship to stress and self-care:

RECOGNIZING YOUR STRESS

When stressed out, type fours may find themselves in the lower side of type two. This can look like extreme displays of emotion as a way to gain sympathy, losing themselves in romantic fantasies, becoming overly clingy with friendships and romantic relationships, or finding themselves too much in need of assistance from other people and wanting to prove that they are actually the one overburdened with helping.

SELF-CARE INFUSION

When you start to feel this way, you have the tools you need to care for yourself. Using the high side of type one, you can create the structure you need to live a balanced life. Showing up every day to a regular routine and with a plan in place for yourself will help you put action to your dreams. This can also be a great way to bring in healthy, supportive habits that will keep you from the deep pit of nursing old wounds as an escape from doing the tasks you need to remain stress-free. Finally, this is often the cure to the cycle of type fours feeling like they want to discover what will make them significant—instead they focus on becoming truly great at something that interests them through disciplined practice of their skill.

RECOGNIZING STAGNATION

In the same way that you can use the preparation and team-building elements of type one to relive stress, you can also go to that place by accident. This can happen in two major ways: First, in allowing your discipline to turn into self-shaming and guilt trips that adopt and amplify the harsh inner critic of type one—instead of following through with your commitments, you set the rules to do so and then shame yourself when you don't follow through. Secondly, the type four, when not paying attention, can accidentally sink into a spirit of elitism—turning your critical eye outward as a way to prove to yourself that you are significant. This can lead type fours to harshly judge the taste, talent, intelligence, and depth of other people while also becoming increasingly unsatisfied with the reality of their life—escaping more into their daydreams of what their life "could" be.

MOTIVATION INFUSION

This is where it's helpful to bring in the high side of type two and take time to intentionally look outside of yourself. It can be incredibly beneficial for type fours to regularly volunteer or serve others in some way. Getting out of your own emotional landscape and seeing the suffering of other people and providing a form of relief can offer reprieve from the constant inner dialogue and lack of self-worth. This can provide a boost to your self-esteem, take you out of a state of self-pity, and show you how simple it is to take action when it's needed.

LEVELS OF HEALTH

HEALTHY

In their healthiest state, type fours find their significance through radical self-acceptance and intentional creative action, finding ways to share their reflections with the world. Their energy is being spent on things that matter to them and, therefore, they have found a way out of self-absorption.

AVERAGE

In most cases, our type fours are afraid that they cannot become great while also maintaining the demands of everyday life. They resent others who are able to pursue their goals and remain stable. The average type four pushes and pulls at his or her relationships, creating a clear desire for time with the other person while also retreating from them to test their commitment. They live in fear that they will never be truly understood and escape to daydreaming that a rescuer will come.

UNHEALTHY

Type fours may find themselves afraid of wasting their lives pushing away things and people that can't handle their emotional demands. They have an idealized version of who they are that they can't live up to and resent both themselves for not being that and others for not seeing them that way. They turn their hatred inward while also resenting others for not helping them.

GETTING H.O.N.E.S.T. FOR TYPE FOUR

What I believe is remarkable about type fours is the way you hold full capacity for the human condition. I believe type fours have more access to the full range of our emotions and the complete depths of who we are. Type fours have an ability to see the world as living art, which can manifest as deep love, true bliss, access to magic, and so much more. To be loved and seen by a type four is a powerful and beautiful thing that I think we all could benefit from. A type four can make a plant, a building, or a human feel like poetry. In addition, there is no one I want more by my side during a season of darkness than a type four—someone who isn't afraid of what I've become but instead knows the feeling well and can hold the space with me while I express whatever it is that comes forward.

What is equally heartbreaking for me is that with all of this magic, the type four is still not quite satisfied with life as it is. There's a constant awareness of what they are lacking both internally and circumstantially—so much so that, in a way, there is no rest. There is such a desire to be found as significant that they forget to notice all of the significance that is boiling right there inside of them. I crave for our type fours to know that in just being, they are carrying the key to their significance. I think what is particularly tricky and baffling is that I know that some part of our type fours knows it. You know that deep down you are special. You just feel you have to prove it through some sort of skill or achievement or the intensity of your suffering. Sometimes, significance is greatest in simply being what you are. I believe one of the greatest gifts we can receive from our type fours is surrounding ourselves with people who are simply living in such a way that the world is magic and our feelings are all OK.

HONOR YOUR STRENGTHS

The first step is to take time to get really honest with yourself about what makes you amazing. Celebrate all of the elements of your personality that you love. If it's tricky for you to think of things you love about yourself, consider what you do and who you are that contributes positively to the world around you. If you hear yourself say "nothing," this is a good time to practice pushing past that voice and intentionally looking and asking the people in your life to help you see them as well.

A few things that are amazing about type fours:
- You are comfortable with the range of human expression.
- You are empathetic.
- You are full of depth.
- You are creative.
- You are often aesthetically gifted.
- You are a great support to those who suffer.
- You are interesting and curious.
- You are filled with rich love.
- You are introspective.
- You are significant simply by being the way you are in the world.

It's important that you know the goal isn't to avoid being a type four. You don't need to reject everything that you are—even your strengths. It's simply about holding the awareness for what is keeping you away from your essence. It's OK that your good qualities are part of your type pattern—it doesn't make them less good.

Take some time to write out your personal strengths below.

_____

_____

_____

_____

_____

OPEN YOUR EYES TO BLIND SPOTS

When I started writing this chapter, it felt hard to discuss some of the struggles of type fours. I told my type four husband, "I feel like that's all just so much for you to carry." That's when I realized that, for him, it's what he's been carrying his whole life. He's not afraid of the darkness, but I am. In fact, that's why connection with type fours is so valuable to the rest of us, as it helps us not to be afraid of the dark.

This is the section where we run through all of the things that you will want to hold space for while you grow—the things that are habitual but aren't truly serving you in the pursuit of a life where you get to fully express your truest essence. In this, I want to let you know that a couple of these are going to be in direct contradiction to how you've traditionally viewed the world. It may, quite frankly, piss you off. But know that I write these things in love, and that I didn't make them up. (They're integrated ancient Enneagram teachings.) You are in the driver's seat of your growth journey. At the end of the day, you decide how much of this is right for you.

A few things to keep in mind as a type four:

1. You aren't different from the rest of us.
As children, type fours felt both rejected by their caregivers and fundamentally different from their family of origin. Not only did they feel different, they felt as though they were the problem. This can lead to a feeling of constant inferiority, separation, and isolation. While we all need to do work around healing our relationships to the way we were raised, I think it's particularly important for type fours. Take the time not to need to feel superior to those people as a way not to feel rejected. Instead, find a place inside of yourself where they simply are what they are, you are not wrong for feeling different from them, and they are not wrong for being different from you. While it can be tempting to linger in the space of regret that your childhood didn't support you in the way you craved, it's important that you realize that none of ours did.

Every human was born into a flawed and ineffective family. The majority of Enneagram schools believe we were born with our type, and we grew up with a heightened awareness to what we were already sensitive. Yes, your family couldn't do you justice, and that's OK! Allowing yourself to see yourself as just as human as the rest of us will give you the power not to cave when hard things come your way. It will release you from a very comfortable and familiar excuse to stay small.

The last thing the world needs is for one of our greatest teachers of humanity to remain stunted, silenced, and ineffective. Your voice is important, and the belief that you are outside of the regular human experience is silencing.

2. Learning not to treat your feelings as facts will lead to healthier relationships.

This is perhaps the point I'm most aware could lead our type fours to rage and burn this book. Of course, all feelings are valid, and we are all worthy of being heard in the truest form of our emotions. However, our emotions are simply stories. We experience the world through all of our past wounds, fears, prejudices, and preconceived ideas of what will happen to us, who we are, and how people feel about us. When you are someone who fundamentally believes you are misunderstood, inferior, unworthy, and essentially the worst kind of person, guess how you're going to interpret the world?

Have you ever had the confusing conversation with someone where they really hurt your feelings and you say to them, "You told me I was worthless and a loser and terrible at my job!" and they respond, "That's not what I said. What I said was, 'Can you grab me that cup and put it over here?'" These conversations happen because we interpret the words of another person through the lens of what we already believe about ourselves. When we take the time to separate our emotions from the story, we are more able to see what really happened.

Instead of the story being: "I was getting ready for the date, and they came into the room and started telling me how long it's taking me to get ready, that they didn't like my clothes, and they acted like they didn't even want to be married to me in the first place."

We realize it's actually: "They came into the room and asked me if I was already dressed and how much longer I thought it would take me to get ready."

In the process of doing this work, you may need to take time to ask the other person, "What did you mean when you asked if this is what I was wearing? Do you like this outfit?" This will give the person the chance to tell you what he or she means instead of the story being written by your inner self-doubt. The hardest part is that you have to trust that they mean what they say when they say it. The rest of us think you're pretty awesome. We're just out here waiting for you to know it too.

3. Separating yourself from your struggle will set you free.
For type fours, the relationship with struggle and pain is a very cozy and very comfortable safety blanket. It's the thing that can offer you everything your animalistic desires crave. It's proof that you are special, flawed, and fatally wounded so you can't be who you thought you were going to be. It's proof that you can give up.

To move into the truest essence of who you are and what is available to you, you have to release attachment to suffering. Depending on your subtype, the work may be admitting to yourself that you don't have to suffer; it may be not nursing your wounds for long periods of time and using your suffering as an excuse not to be and do more; or it may be releasing the need to find revenge for past suffering in your life.

No matter which relationship to suffering you are engaged with, freedom is on the other side of breaking up with suffering. You don't have to be in a long-term relationship with your pain. Your pain doesn't define you.

4. We all mess up every single day.
For a lot of type fours, it can feel as though other people aren't out here struggling—that they wake up and live these perfect lives where things come together for them, and they are more capable and charming and qualified. With this belief, when a type four makes a mistake, isn't immediately gifted at a new skill, or receives negative feedback, it can feel like they might as well just give up because they always get things wrong.

I'm gonna let you in on a little secret right now, and it's that I mess up every single day. Every day! Every single day, I drop the ball on something in my business, have a typo in something I put online, hurt the feelings of someone I love, or make awkward conversation with the checkout guy and leave feeling embarrassed. Every day. This isn't some fatal flaw—it's life.

The only difference between those who do amazing things and those who don't is their relationship to failure when they fail. It's acknowledging that failure is inevitable and then just learning what you can from it and moving forward.

If you let mistakes get you down, we miss out on what you have to share, and you are more likely to end up in a cycle of daydreaming of living someone else's life instead of making magic with your own. Which brings us to . . .

5. Nothing outside of yourself will ever make you feel happier.
There is a very sneaky little temptation that comes up for our type fours, and that's their vice—envy. It can be so tantalizing to look at the

lives of other people, see what they have, and believe that it's better than what you have. To look at their talent, their marriage, their home, or their career and believe that you won't be truly happy until . . .

That sentence, "I will be happy when . . ." is one that I want to be an alarm in your mind. It signifies that you're leaning into a part of yourself that doesn't have your best interest at heart. That little sentence is an alarm that you are seeking your completion in the world outside of yourself.

True satisfaction, the kind that will stick by you even when nothing is working out, is built from getting really cozy with exactly what is. It comes from being fully unapologetic about what you bring to the table, who you are, and how you work. It comes from seeing yourself as equal to others who are also worthy of good things. It comes from enjoying your life even in the mess of it.

Type fours have the most amazing capacity to find beauty in everything—every little moment and every little experience. Tapping into this will serve you beautifully over the course of your life.

NOTE YOUR SUPPORT PLAN

This is the part of the process where we get to talk about finding what actually serves YOU when it comes to creating a life that you love. This is very exciting for me to share with type fours because so often type fours get caught up in self-doubt and struggle to create a life that matches the world they envision for themselves in their mind.

So, how do we learn to take the action required to build the life you feel destined to have? For our type fours, I say to start with two main questions: "What mundane tasks am I avoiding out of fear of being average?" and "What negative feedback or experiences am I holding on to that make me feel like I can't move forward?"

Below, you will find a list of things that may support you in the process of releasing shame, creating a healthy routine, and pushing through self-doubt.

A few things that may support you in the process:
- Determine a small morning routine that you can do before each day, as well as a simple "wind-down" routine before you go to sleep at night.
- Go to bed and wake up at the same time every day.
- Surround yourself with people who inspire you and believe in you.
- Write things that you feel shame about on a piece of paper and burn the paper.
- Share your honest doubts, fears, shame, and insecurities with someone you trust and let them love you for who you are.
- Practice a "Ten Good Things List"—this is my antidote to a gratitude list. Gratitude lists can feel stuffy, stale, and artificial. A "Ten Good Things List" is simply the first ten things you think of that make you happy.
- Take a complaint break. Give yourself a day or a week where you intentionally attempt to focus on what is going "right" instead of what is missing.
- Perform regular exercise, which will be your best friend. Get out in nature, see the beauty of the world, and get those endorphins pumping! The most important thing here is that it is a habit, not an obligation, and establishes a relationship to exercise that is pleasurable in nature and not guilt-tripping.

What can you do this week to get develop a healthy routine for yourself?

EXPLORE YOUR RELATIONSHIPS

So far, you've honored your strengths, gotten really honest with yourself about your blind spots, and set aside a plan of support in the process. Now it's time to talk about relationships. It's all well and good to do all of this work on our own, but what do we do when someone else comes in and disrupts our perfect synchronicity of self-compassion? This is where we get to explore what you bring into your relationships. What do you positively contribute? What do you do that doesn't serve your work to being the warm, generous, loving, and accepting person that you are in your essence?

Beautiful things that type fours bring to their relationships:
- Holding space for us when we are at our darkest.
- Helping us see the small, beautiful moments in life.
- Encouraging us to slow down and take it all in.
- Romancing us.
- You're intelligent and interesting.
- Creating beautiful experiences with us.
- Giving us permission to be human.
- Being deep and passionate and engaging.

A few things that may not be serving your relationships:
- The push/pull pattern is common for type fours—pushing someone away just enough to ask them please not to leave. In a similar way, they want desperately to connect to people and be accepted by them but don't really want to go out and get to know people.
- Criticism can be hard for type fours. If you are not working on loving yourself when someone has feedback for you, it can feel like they're kicking you while you are down. Healthy relationships thrive when you are able to safely discuss your wants and needs. When a type four isn't in a good place, they can shut down this

space with their rejection of feedback and a desperate need to prove it isn't true.

- Emotional volatility.
- Self-absorbed behavior patterns, such as forgetting to ask the people in your life questions about themselves or entering into monologues about how you feel about things without checking in to see if the other person is being heard.
- You prioritize the way you feel over everything else.
- You attempt to connect through the identity you are cultivating instead of who you truly are.
- You disqualify people if they don't totally see you as you see yourself.
- You believe the stories you write about interactions you have with people instead of what they tell you they feel about you.

The reason we're talking about this—even if it's uncomfortable and sometimes painful—is because in the long run it will bring you so much relief. Holding the truth that both of these lists exist simultaneously is the key to ease in your relationships. Knowing what you can control and what isn't yours to worry about can be an extremely relaxing move to make. That tiny list up there, that's it. Think about that! You are doing so much right!

Take a few minutes to think of your own lists. Write down what you personally bring to your relationships, both positively and negatively.

Now, take a few moments here to think of the three most important relationships in your life. Write out how you would like for them to feel. How would they change if you could imagine a world where they were exactly as you hoped?

What about your lists would need to shift in order to have the relationships that you want?

SOFTEN YOUR PATH

OK, so we've established what makes you amazing. (Way to go, by the way!) We've covered what areas of your life may be in need of some tender love and care. We've even discussed how to support yourself in this growth. Let's now talk about how we're going to keep this process going even when it feels difficult or impossible or a bit too unnatural.

I want to give you these four soft internal shifts to make—just four things to hold on to each and every day that will help you in the work of being your healthiest type four self.

1. Facts, not feelings.

In any given situation when you feel the need to rear up, hide away, or shut down, ask yourself if what's upsetting you are the facts or your feelings. Check in with the reality of what happened and what it brought up in you. Let your feelings have their time to tell you what they're experiencing, and then give them full permission to rest. They did their job of bringing to your attention that something was triggered, but they aren't needed anymore. Form your opinion of the situation based solely out of the facts, not what you perceive the facts to mean about you.

2. I am not uniquely flawed, and no one else thinks I am either.

When something goes wrong or you feel overly criticized, repeat to yourself the following phrase, "I am not uniquely flawed, and no one else thinks I am either." The intention of this is to release you of the shame that you are the only one who doesn't get everything right, without needing to prove that to other people by arguing their point or convincing yourself that you are superior to them. Humans make mistakes. Life is life and we all move on.

3. The one thing

When life feels like "too much" and you aren't sure how you're going to make it through this task or the day, just do one thing. Pick one thing that will take you a step closer to where you're trying to go. Whether that is learning a new skill, making it through a tough transition, or doing the work of the Enneagram, commit to just one thing. After that one thing, you can call it finished or you can do one more thing—that's up to you.

4. Pride pad

If you do nothing else from our chapter together, I encourage you to pick up this new habit. Keep a pad of paper beside your bed, and at the end of every single day, write down one thing you are proud of yourself for from that day. At times, you may think there's nothing you're proud of, but you must force yourself to think of something. It can be as big as "being a great parent" or as small as "I used a reusable water bottle today instead of buying plastic." Build this into a habit, and after a while you'll have a place to go when you start to doubt what kind of person you are. A log of all the good things you've done over the last little while is a balm for the wounds you've been nursing for far too long.

TURN THAT INTO SOMETHING BEAUTIFUL

Creativity is important for all types. It's important especially for our type fours, who seem to have been born with a deep desire to make something of significance to share with the world. I encourage you to make this a personal practice before taking it public, but feel safe to share with the world before you think you're ready. You're likely ready to share way sooner than you feel you are.

So, what do you, as a type four, need to keep in mind when it comes to creativity?

- Don't give up at the first disruption. We all hit roadblocks, so keep going!
- You don't have to feel like it in order to sit down and work on it. It can be really helpful for type fours to commit to showing up every single day and doing the work. It can be tempting to wait until you feel motivated or inspired, but you will get much further in the process if you just show up at the same time every day and participate.
- No one is great without practice. All truly gifted people failed and practiced and failed and practiced. If you want to be great, you will be committing yourself to a life of practice. Prepare for that now and don't get discouraged when you pick a new hobby and aren't immediately gifted.
- You don't have to wait to feel worthy in order to start. There is no permission slip for being creative. No one is guarding the gates, waiting for your proof of credentials. You are innately qualified.
- Be cautious of nursing old wounds as proof that you will fail. It can be tempting for type fours to hold on to a Rolodex of all of the times they've failed before and use it as proof that failure is always around the corner. Doing so increases the risk that you will not follow through and, therefore, add another "failure" to your Rolodex.
- There are no original ideas, and this isn't the time for that anyway. You will never be the first person to participate in your potential creative outlet. When you are beginning, that is the time to learn from those who have come before you. Of course, you will eventually make it your own. However, don't get caught up in knowing how to do that before you even start. Learn the skill first, then focus on finding out how you will add your own spin to it.

Dear Four

Writing you this letter is an honor for me—to have the chance to shine a little bit of light onto the beauty that you possess is a joy.

Here's the thing: I believe that type fours change the world, I truly do. I believe we give a lot of credit to the more action-oriented types, but we forget that so many great turns in history began because there were people who felt "different." They saw the world in ways that didn't try to cover up the darkness and weren't afraid to talk about what it brought up in them. They didn't shy away from the truth of how they felt.

I think some of the greatest work that type fours do is taking the time to get really honest with themselves about how they feel and what they've experienced, and then sharing that with the world in such a way that we're all changed for having seen it. This is inside of you. Innately, you are perfectly suited, just as you are, to reflect and share.

The challenge is going to be creating a safe space for yourself to learn the skills and do the things to get your work from inside your head out into the world. I challenge you to treat yourself a bit like you would a child who is learning to tie his or her shoes for the first time. You wouldn't watch them and yell, "You're messing it up! You're not doing it right! You're never going to get this!" Why not? Because this is the swiftest way for you to demotivate their progress. They will surely give up. Instead, you celebrate all of the small achievements with them along the way, you slow down and teach them again, you expect them to practice before they get it right, and when they're confused, you show them again. Give that same presence and grace to yourself, and you will thrive!

THINKER

OBSERVER

INVESTIGATOR

SOUND COUNSEL

Type Five

"I know that I will be OK as long as I have
something that I've truly mastered."

"Did you know that . . .?"	A room in your house that's just for you.	Only books for presents, please.	Has inside jokes with themselves	Remembers what someone wore two years ago
Niche interests.	Forgets that they have an actual human body and aren't just a brain	Seriously, being alone.	"I'll think about that and get back to you."	"No, that's not right."
Documentaries.	Spoiler alerts.	5	Minimalism.	"Why?"
A robust savings account.	Knows the origins of everything they're interested in	Feels awkward AF	"I'll take care of myself, you take care of yourself."	Known for a specific set of knowledge.
People-watching.	Probably doesn't read/follow us on Instagram	Feels out of this world	Believes in aliens	Dreams of a utopian society

HOW YOU CONFUSE OTHERS

By Enneagram type.

1 - EXPECTING OTHERS TO DO THINGS THE WAY YOU WOULD DO THEM.

2 - EXPECTING OTHERS TO ANTICIPATE YOUR NEEDS WITHOUT THEM BEING EXPRESSED.

3 - EXPECTING OTHERS TO CHASE THEIR DREAMS WITH THE SAME FERVOR THAT YOU CHASE YOURS.

4 - EXPECTING OTHERS TO SHARE IN THE PERFECT ROMANTIC EXPERI-ENCE THAT THEY MAY NOT KNOW IS SUPPOSED TO BE ROMANTIC.

5 - EXPECTING OTHERS NOT TO MISS YOU WHEN YOU'RE GONE.

6 - EXPECTING OTHERS TO LIVE UP TO YOUR EXPECTATIONS OF WHAT IT MEANS TO BE A GOOD AUTHORITY FIGURE.

7 - EXPECTING OTHERS TO MOVE ON WITH THEIR LIVES WHEN YOU'VE DECIDED TO MOVE ON WITH YOURS.

8 - EXPECTING OTHERS NOT TO GET OFFENDED BY THE "TRUTH" AS YOU SEE IT.

9 - EXPECTING OTHERS TO BE OK WITH NEVER TALKING ABOUT YOUR PROBLEMS.

@enneagramandcoffee

ABOUT TYPE FIVE

Basic desire: "It's important to me that I am capable, competent, and informed."

Basic fear: "I most fear being helpless, useless, or overwhelmed."

Type fives are analytical, observant, and insightful. Type fives often felt as if they were either unable to get their needs met by their caregivers or were consumed by the presence of their families of origin. This developed a sense that a type five would need to meet their own needs in private through holding on to their resources. Type fives are intentional about managing both their resources and their energy levels, not so much out of selfishness or stinginess but more so out of a belief that this is what is necessary to survive. Type fives hold a continued awareness of this and make decisions to prevent depletion.

There is also a drive to understand the world—a need to know the intricacies of life from all angles, timelines, and explanations.

These two pieces often play together in someone who lives life through the safety of their mind. They experience the world through research, thought, and curiosity.

Type fives are inquisitive, economical, studious, and self-sufficient, and are likely the most informed people you know.

I titled type fives "Sound Counsel" because they have a gift for looking at the world objectively. They are often very loyal and trustworthy friends whom many rely on for thoughtful feedback. Type fives are particularly helpful when making a decision between two things.

They're good at looking at your options and helping you to think through what would be best for you. They have a true gift for being able to do this free of emotional bias.

Most type fives spend a lot of their time and energy focused on understanding the world around them and learning everything they can about whatever it is they've decided to master. Because of this, a type five can easily become detached from others emotionally. They may engage through a sharing of facts and information and find themselves drawn to connecting primarily with people who have shared interests and similar levels of expertise.

I believe the hardest thing about being a type five is having your natural way of orienting in the world be so misunderstood. I've had many type fives express the feeling that others think they are "aloof" or "off-putting." At the same time, when I work with people who are in relationships with type fives, I receive the feedback that they love their type fives so much and just want more of them—more connection, more time, and a peek behind their walls. The reality is that type fives typically build very high walls between their emotions and their expression.

There isn't a lack of emotion there; rather, it's a hidden emotion, a belief that their sensitivities cannot only be reasoned through, they can also be dealt with on their own. This can lead to patterns of withdrawing to recoup and then entering back into a relationship when they feel available for it.

When this withdrawing happens, many loved ones of our type fives will pursue them more intensely, asking what's wrong and if they did something to upset them—knocking on their walls, which can perpetuate the cycle of type fives feeling that they need to hoard their resources.

A lot of the work for our type fives comes down to not only communicating more intentionally when they take their space but also recognizing when they are retreating or hoarding as a defense mechanism and moving in the direction of non-attachment. It's a belief that they will be supported by life and they can release the constant management of their resources.

SUBTYPES OF TYPE FIVE

The following subtypes of type five are based on the three instinctual variants and how those interact with the type five's relationship to minimizing needs and limiting connection to others. The self-preservation type five focuses on building boundaries, the social type five focuses on following a specific moral code, and the sexual type five focuses on a single partner and the romantic ideal.

SELF-PRESERVATION
- Subtype with the most boundaries
- Clearest example of introversion
- The external world seems hostile, intrusive, and inadequate
- Difficulty with expressing anger—prefer to withdraw instead of communicating
- Private
- Fear becoming dependent on others for support
- May merge with the tone of a group in order not to be seen

SOCIAL
- In pursuit of the meaning of life
- Attach themselves to a set of ideals

- In search of relationships based on shared ideals
- Wants to be someone important and pursues this by aligning with people they admire and connecting intellectually to their ideals
- Has to be cautious of being intellectually spiritual while missing the empathy that is required to reach true enlightenment
- Can look like a type one or seven

SEXUAL
- Focused on finding the ideal partnership
- Places value on one-on-one connection
- Intense, romantic, and emotionally sensitive
- Possesses a rich inner world full of utopian fantasies
- In pursuit of ultimate intimacy—sharing in full transparency and having others share with them in full transparency
- Can look like a type four

TYPE FIVE AND WINGS

As a type five, you can pull from either of your wings to help round out your personality. You may find that you already lean in one direction more than the other. However, you have access to the skills and vices of both wings. Here are some qualities you can borrow from your neighbors:

TYPE FOUR WING
When pulling in this wing, you may find yourself tapping into your curiosity. Use this wing to aid in developing your unique personal vision. You may find yourself becoming increasingly introspective and creative. This wing can make you very whimsical and inventive.

TYPE SIX WING

This wing can aid you in organization as well as help you in becoming more detail-oriented. Tap into this wing for enhanced cooperation with the group, discipline, and work ethic.

TYPE FIVE AND LINES

When in stress, the type five moves to type seven, and when in rest, they move to type eight. With that understanding, here's what you may want to keep in mind in your relationship to stress and self-care:

RECOGNIZING YOUR STRESS

When stressed out, type fives may find themselves in the lower side of type seven. This can look like busying themselves with projects and activities. They may become increasingly scattered as they attempt to find a specific skill or area to master and spread their focus too thin, increasing the agitation of discovering a niche.

SELF-CARE INFUSION

When you start to feel this way, you have the tools you need to care for yourself. Using the high side of type eight, you can take intentional action toward your goals and focus on prioritizing your energy. You learn to listen to your body and get in touch with what it is telling you. This move also allows you to use all of your knowledge to tackle day-to-day real-life problems.

RECOGNIZING STAGNATION

In the same way that you can use the preparation and team-building elements of type eight to relieve stress, you can also go to that place by accident. This can look like being overly self-protective, defensive, and detaching from vulnerability.

MOTIVATION INFUSION

This is where it's helpful to bring in the high side of type seven—allowing yourself to see the good in a given situation or moment and intentionally seeking awareness for the magic of every day and relationship you are invested in. It can also be a helpful tool for putting yourself out there when you feel guarded and allow yourself to be seen and heard.

LEVELS OF HEALTH

HEALTHY

In their healthiest state, type fives become more fully connected with the world around them. They release the idea that they are not one with the world and allow themselves to participate rather than simply observe. They pursue original and creative ideas and often contribute revolutionary inventions to society.

AVERAGE

In most cases, our type fives are afraid that they need more and more research and preparation to be qualified to take action. They are unsure of themselves, fearful of the needs of others, and live with a wall up to protect against the intrusion of others. They minimize their own needs and hoard the resources they have available to them.

UNHEALTHY

Type fives may find themselves fearful of never finding their place in the world. As an act of self-protection, they may cut themselves off from the outside world, rejecting their needs and living in isolation.

GETTING H.O.N.E.S.T. FOR TYPE FIVE

What I believe is remarkable about type fives is the curiosity with which they approach the world—their innate craving for more knowledge, information, and understanding. This is particularly beautiful when applied to a specific area of interest. The depth in which you are able to explore a single topic is remarkable. This creates integrity of information and a dissatisfaction with glossing over the truth. Because of this, and the pickiness that type fives can have when it comes to who they open up to and when they share their energy, I find type fives to be one of the most trustworthy of all the types. They have an ability to separate themselves from the facts and lead with information that I find relaxing to engage with.

In addition, type fives are generally not people who take advantage of others for their own gain. In fact, the work for most type fives is in accepting the ability to take anything at all from anyone. With all of this in consideration, I believe type fives to be one of the most truly trustworthy and loving of all the types. Type fives rarely have ulterior motives when giving or fib the facts, which are such admirable qualities.

What is equally heartbreaking for me is that all of this information, beautiful authentic love to be shared, great advice, and wisdom are so often unseen. The type fives' fear of limited resources can lead them to hide themselves from the world, often keeping incredible talents under wraps for years or lifetimes. Always afraid of connection or overly relying on others, type fives can have difficulty opening up and sharing their friendship and love with new people.

This can go as far as type fives believing that they don't want those connections. However, there is so much lost when we live inside the echo chamber of our own minds. In this process, type fives are limiting the information, perspective, and, ultimately, true wisdom that can be obtained throughout the course of their lives.

HONOR YOUR STRENGTHS

The first step is to take time to get really honest with yourself about what makes you amazing. Celebrate all of the elements of your personality that you love. If it's tricky for you to think of things you love about yourself, consider what you do and who you are that contributes positively to the world around you.

A few things that are amazing about type fives:
- You understand things in-depth.
- You are logical and unbiased.
- You bring high standards for research.
- You are self-reliant.
- You are trustworthy.
- You are great at holding space for the emotions of others without getting swept up in them yourself.
- You are decisive.
- You are observant.
- You are original.
- You are incredibly capable and informed.

It's important that you know the goal isn't to avoid being a type five. You don't need to reject everything that you are—even your strengths. It's simply about holding the awareness for what is keeping you away from your essence. It's OK that your good qualities are part of your type pattern—it doesn't make them less good.

Take some time to write out your personal strengths below.

_____

_____

_____

_____

_____

OPEN YOUR EYES TO BLIND SPOTS

This can be a tricky conversation to have. For many type fives, the vices that you carry are believed to be "the way life is"—or simply, facts. I want to encourage you to approach this with an open mind and a willingness to explore. While it can be tempting to live a life deep in your mind, you may be missing out on some of the wisdom that you are seeking.

This is the section where we run through all of the things that you will want to hold space for while you grow—the things that are habitual but aren't truly serving you in the pursuit of a life where you get to fully express your truest essence. In this, I want to let you know that a couple of these are going to be in direct contradiction with how you've traditionally viewed the world. It may, quite frankly, piss you off. But know that I write these things in love, and that I didn't make them up. (They're integrated ancient Enneagram teachings.) You are in the driver's seat of your growth journey—at the end of the day you decide how much of this is right for you.

A few things to keep in mind as a type five:

1. You do not have limited resources and energy.
As children, type fives felt as if their resources were constantly limited or in danger of being depleted. They grew up learning to hide and isolate as a way of protecting what they needed to survive. When we

carry this into adulthood, it can become a form of perceived control to hoard time, energy, and resources as a method of self-protection. Operating from a place of scarcity is a quick way to keep your voice silenced, your finances tight, and your reach small.

You are not a cup of water that, once consumed, is empty forever. You are a water tap that can turn on and pour out effortlessly and turn off intentionally. You do not have to hide yourself away and close people off to protect your resources. You have other options.

Communicate your needs thoughtfully and kindly, take your time away intentionally and not habitually, and know what you want to get out of that time you're taking. Do you need ideas, rest, and time to think? Is there a need at all, or are you just used to feeling like you don't have enough? Take all of that great curiosity that you have for the world and turn it inward when the desire to retreat arises.

The reason this is important is that your mind is too bright and too interesting to hide those thoughts away. The world benefits when you share, and—whether you are one hundred percent on board with this idea yet or not—so do you!

2. You cannot truly detach from emotions.

Type fives are the least emotionally expressive of all the types. It's like there's a thick castle wall between where you think and where you feel. This doesn't mean that you aren't sensitive, though. I know you don't have to be told this because you can feel it. But it's important to communicate that you can't truly ever avoid your emotional being.

Our emotions linger around us when we aren't processing them. They come out in strange and unexpected ways. They may cause physical symptoms, a desire to hermit up, and unspoken tensions in relationships.

It's important that your feelings be felt. Practice holding space for your emotions in your body. This will connect you more deeply to the human experience, aid you in communicating your message, and create healthier, more sustainable relationships with others.

3. Those walls may not be serving you long-term.
I know that you like to believe that you don't need much and that there isn't a hole where relationships should be in your life. There is truly something beautiful about not needing anyone but simply wanting them. However, when your desire not to "need" evolves and morphs into deciding not to "want," that's where we have a bit of a sticky situation.

People thrive in community. Studies have shown that people in a community experience increased happiness, lower rates of suicide, longer life expectancy, and higher likelihood of financial success. That's not to mention the spiritual and emotional intelligence that we gain from engaging with other people who challenge, question, and refine us.

I'm not telling you to run out your front door, open your arms, and yell, "Everyone is welcome!" Of course not. I'm simply saying be open to new people, don't hide away from those who love you, and maybe share about five percent more of yourself with the world here and there. There is nothing quite like being fully known and loved anyway.

Yes, there is potential rejection, but you heal from that. It goes pretty quickly, to be honest. And the reward of true acceptance is so worth that risk!

4. You don't have to do this alone.
You know how to take care of yourself. In fact, you're likely quite good
at it. It's amazing that you don't have to learn that skill as so many
other people do. However, you don't have to do it all alone.

There are times when it would benefit you greatly to open yourself up
to help from other people.

When you let others support you, you open yourself up not only to
more love but also the ability to do more with increased accuracy.

5. Taking action needs to happen before you feel "ready."
One of the really amazing things about type fives is that you are
careful not to speak on a topic unless you are fully informed. You
take your time, you do your research, and are slow to call yourself an
expert. However, all of that research without action is simply an act
of self-indulgence. To take that research and turn it into something
that positively contributes to the world—that will require stepping out
and taking the risk that you are ready even before you feel it. There is
no limit to the amount of research you could do, and there is always
more to learn. Decide what being an "expert" on that particular topic
looks like to you, consider what you would need to know to claim
the right to take action, and then allow that to be your guidepost.
Otherwise, you could find yourself in an endless cycle of researching
to learn just enough to know you have more to research.

NOTE YOUR SUPPORT PLAN
This is the part of the process where we get to talk about finding what
actually serves YOU when it comes to creating a life that you love.
This is very exciting for me to share with type fives because so often
type fives may find that their fear of being uninformed can prevent
them from having experiences that make them feel alive.

So, how do we learn to take the action required to build a life that is just as rich as your inner world? For our type fives, I encourage you to begin with this question: "What am I afraid will happen if I open up my world and give from my resources?"

Below, you will find a list of things that may support you in the process of creating meaningful connections, expressing your vulnerability, and finding a place of embodiment.

- Choose one or two people with whom you take intentional time to share your truth. Be open and vulnerable with them on a regular basis.
- Have a filter for why you're taking time. Determine a clear indicator that you are taking time intentionally and not avoiding something else.
- Set a deadline for research—not necessarily a time deadline, but more a level of knowledge that means you are fully informed.
- Practice asking yourself, "Where do I feel that in my body?" when you are experiencing emotions.
- Ask for one thing you need each day.
- Express gratitude for your closest relationships in specific detail and on a regular basis.
- Get into some form of embodiment practice, such as meditation, yoga, or dance—anything that will take you out of your mind and put you into your body.
- Take time to intentionally practice empathy. Get curious about the experience of other people and attempt to feel what they're feeling.

What can you do this week to contribute to your opening and embodiment?

EXPLORE YOUR RELATIONSHIPS

So far, you've honored your strengths, gotten really honest with yourself about your blind spots, and set aside a plan of support in the process. Now it's time to talk about relationships. It's all well and good to do all of this work on our own but what do we do when someone else comes in disrupts our perfect synchronicity of self-compassion? This is where we get to explore what you bring into your relationships. What do you positively contribute? What do you do that doesn't serve your work to being the connected, capable, and curious person that you are in your essence?

Beautiful things that type fives bring to their relationships:
- Bringing a logical perspective.
- Not breaking when we are falling apart. You hold space without becoming overwhelmed by our emotions.
- Reminding us to do our research and not to take the world at face value.
- Paying attention.
- Bringing interesting and new ideas to the table.
- Giving great advice.
- Self-sufficiency.

A few things that may not be serving your relationships:
- Isolating yourself.
- Avoiding conflict.
- "I'll take care of me and you take care of you."
- Integrated connection.
- The illusion of control.

The reason we're talking about this—even if it's uncomfortable and sometimes painful—is because in the long run, it will bring you so much relief. Holding the truth that both of these lists exist simultaneously is the key to ease in your relationships. Knowing what you can control and what isn't yours to worry about can be an extremely relaxing move to make. That tiny list up there, that's it. Think about that! You are doing so much right!

Take a few minutes to think of your own lists. Write down what you personally bring to your relationships, both positively and negatively.

Now, take a few moments here to think of the three most important relationships in your life. Write out how you would like for them to feel. How would they change if you could imagine a world where they were exactly as you hoped?

What about your lists would need to shift in order to have the relationships that you want?

SOFTEN YOUR PATH

OK, so we've established what makes you amazing. (Way to go, by the way!) We've covered what areas of your life may be in need of some tender love and care. We've even discussed how to support yourself in this growth. Let's now talk about how we're going to keep this process going even when it feels difficult or impossible or a bit too unnatural.

I want to give you these four soft internal shifts to make. Just four things to hold on to each and every day that will help you in the work of being your healthiest type five self:

1. Get into your body.

Of all of the Enneagram types, it is easiest for type fives to escape into their minds and to almost forget that the world outside of their heads is relevant. "Getting into your body" is about integrating all of that information into daily practices that will ultimately make you not only physically healthier but also emotionally more engaged. When it comes to a simple practice that you could do every day to engage in this process, I would encourage you to practice yoga nidra, which lets you scan and assess what your body has to tell you!

2. Get curious about your actions.

When you want to retreat or hide out, find yourself pulling away from people, or have a desire to debate someone on a topic, you should pause, get curious, and seek out what is behind that behavior. What are you afraid of? What are you trying to avoid? Is there an emotion under the surface that is being ignored?

3. Exercise your empathy muscle.

Creating a language and a physicality for the feelings of others will help you not only create the substance behind your spiritual practices but also aid you in deeper connections with others. At times, it can seem like connecting intellectually is enough. However, bonds and lasting relationships are built through shared vulnerability. Finding the place within yourself that can deeply empathize with others will help you also empathize with yourself and share when you're in need of support. Bringing your emotions into the picture will only deepen your experience with humanity and give you a more well-rounded and integrated path to relationships.

4. Create an abundance practice.

Count the leaves on the trees, notice angel types (e.g., 333, 444, 555, etc.), look for signs from the universe, or count ten beautiful things all around you when you feel scarcity arise—any practice that helps you notice the abundance of the universe. Take note of the everflowing resources that you see around you. This will aid in releasing the desire to hold tightly to your resources. Recognizing that what goes out often comes back in—in multiples—will help you share more and, therefore, create more impact and develop deeper relationships.

TURN THAT INTO SOMETHING BEAUTIFUL

Creativity is important for all types. But I think it's particularly important for type fives to take all of this incredible, rich thinking and put it into something tangible. It is another practice of getting out of your mind and into the world.

So, what do you, as a type five, need to keep in mind when it comes to creativity?

- You don't have to know everything before you start. Treat it as play for a while and learn as you go.
- It's OK to keep it as a private practice until you're ready to share.
- Sharing will ultimately be an incredibly healing and expanding experience for you.
- Treat creation as experimentation. Get curious about what would happen if you played in this way or that. Don't get hung up on technicalities.
- While it's great to know the history of what you are making and what you are engaging in, I caution you not to use that as a replacement for the creation process. While connected, it does not offer the same benefits to you.
- Give yourself full permission to be "weird" about it. You have incredibly original and unique thoughts. Don't feel pressured to put yourself in a box. Just let this be what it is for you and see where that takes you.

Dear Five

I had a hard time writing your chapter. I think it comes from the place of understanding why you interact with the world the way you do. I get why you would want to be self-sufficient and informed. It seems so harmless and straightforward. It took a lot of reflection for me to realize what is lost on the other side of that.

There is richness and meaning in vulnerable connection to others. One of the struggles of type fives is the search for meaning in the world. If that meaning isn't found, it can feel like the world is, therefore, meaningless and all of this is for nothing. As I meditated on that understanding, I realized that, while it may be a comfortable place not to need others, it isn't always a meaningful place.

So much of our lives can easily be lived in an echo chamber of our own thoughts. Yes, holding it in and reflecting on it can offer up some insight. But the quickest way to integrated understanding is through having conversations with people who push you and question you.

Even more meaningful is taking the time to share who you really are with someone else, being seen in your vulnerabilities and your truth, and letting someone love you even in your failures and your shortcomings. This is what life is about. This is what we all are constantly searching for.

I encourage you to explore what it means to open up to someone or a couple of people. Dance with raw vulnerability and bring your emotions into your life at least once a day.

You have so much rich and interesting insight to share. Don't hold back from authentic connection. It robs us all of your brilliance.

LOYALIST

SKEPTIC

GUARDIAN

TRUSTED
INTEGRATOR

Type Six

"I know that I will be OK as long as I know what
is expected of me and make a point to follow
through with those expectations."

"Do you think I should?"	Group activities.	Worst-case Scenarios.	Seeks the truth in all scenarios	BFFL.
"I'm not sure about them."	Fox News or NPR.	"What if this is the thing that breaks us up?"	"Do you mean that?"	Amazing in a crisis.
Doesn't know what to order for lunch	Rom-coms.	6	Themed parties.	Shares clothes with friends
"Why are they being so nice to me?"	Stands by people a bit longer than may be good for them	Great at giving advice, terrible at listening to their own advice.	Loyal AF.	"I don't know, my plate is already pretty full."
Follows through with their commitments	"I don't want to be the boss, but I'd really like to hire the boss."	Second-guesses the teacher	"No new friends."	Devil's advocate.

BAD FLIRTING TECHNIQUES

By Enneagram type.

1 - "IF YOU WOULD JUST CHANGE THIS ONE THING ABOUT YOURSELF, THEN YOU'D BE PERFECT."

2 - "I KNOW WE JUST MET TODAY BUT, WOULD YOU LIKE ME TO MAKE YOU SOUP?"

3 - "I'VE TAKEN IT UPON MYSELF TO WRITE UP YOUR FIVE-YEAR PLAN."

4 - "SHH, CLOSE YOUR EYES AND LISTEN TO THIS SONG."

5 - "DID YOU KNOW THAT LOVE IS ACTUALLY A CHEMICAL REACTION IN YOUR BRAIN . . ."

6 - "HOW DO I KNOW THAT YOU MEAN WHAT YOU'RE SAYING THOUGH?"

7 - "WANT TO SEE ME LIGHT MY HAND ON FIRE?"

8 - "LISTEN, I NEED TO KNOW IF I'M WASTING MY TIME HERE."

9 - "I GUESS WE CAN MAKE IT OFFICIAL . . . YEAH, I THINK THAT SOUNDS GOOD. WHY NOT?"

@enneagramandcoffee

ABOUT TYPE SIX

Basic Desire: "It's important to me that I feel secure and supported."

Basic Fear: "I am fearful of being left out on my own; that I will be without support and guidance and won't be able to survive without it."

Type sixes are aware, loyal, and hardworking. As children, type sixes often felt as if they were unsafe and didn't have adequate protection. They learned from a young age to keep their eyes open to potential threats as a way never to get caught off guard. Type sixes have a conflicted relationship with authority. While there is a comfort found in having a system or a group to which they belong—a place where they always know what's expected of them—there is also a rebellion to authority, which they do not trust or respect. Type sixes are constantly aware of potential threats or loss of safety. This can look like skepticism of new people and awareness of physical or financial threats. While I wouldn't say that type sixes are walking around frantic, anxious, and uneasy, I would say they are walking around with eyes wide open to what is present and what could be present in the future or hidden between the lines of what is being shared.

Type sixes are prepared, community-oriented, reliable, engaging, and likely some of the most courageous people you know.

I titled type six "Trusted Integrator" because, of all the types I think we need on our team, type six is at the top. As a business owner, I'm always on the lookout for someone who will help my fast-moving brain slow down and think things through—to run my ideas through a series of risk assessments so that we can be proactive about covering our bases. This is what our type sixes do for us in life. They hold awareness for what we all need to remain safe and secure, and they take the necessary action to ensure that we're all taken care of. I like to think of the type six's relationship to authority as a necessary testing of those in charge—the person who makes sure that the ones holding the wheel are actually intending to get us all there safely. That's where trusted comes into play as well. Rarely are type sixes acting out of their own interests alone. Instead, they operate in integrity of what will truly benefit the group. To be in the life of a type six is a special and cherished thing that we shouldn't take for granted.

Most type sixes spend a lot of their time and energy focused on the reality of potential threats. What could come in and disrupt the present equilibrium, and how can I prepare for or prevent that experience? With this awareness, there's also a struggle with their inner authority—a discomfort with trusting their own instinct and operating system. They may seek feedback on their decisions and ideas from several close friends before committing to one. It takes time to earn the trust of a type six. There's a proving process that often takes place. This can happen with people, ideas, systems, plans, or big life decisions. However, once something or someone passes the initial phase of questioning, the type six is fully on board. Once you prove your integrity or the integrity of the plan to a type six, you will have a loyal friend/teammate for life—someone who will get in the trenches with you to make it all come to life.

When I think of what is hardest about being a type six, I imagine it may be the relationship you have to our own inner authority—the constant self-doubting and self-questioning. Not only because it could slow you down in the pursuit of doing the things you want to do in the world but also because it's a hard thing to explain to the people in your life. It's not uncommon for type sixes to rely on the feedback of friends or family when making choices in their life and to seek multiple perspectives before committing to a decision. It comes from a place of thoughtfulness of not wanting to make frivolous or not well-thought-out decisions. That makes sense. However, it can be just enough of a hindrance in your path to keep you from doing fun, rewarding, and life-giving activities. Not to mention, it gives a bit too much authority to the people in your life. At the end of the day, only you know what is best for you. Every other perspective is going to be found wanting because they don't have all of the information.

A lot of the work for our type sixes comes down to learning to trust their intuition and living in the present moment. Intentionally choosing to trust that you know what is best for yourself can help you have more ease in relationships, experience more of what will give you life, and help you spend more time living and less time thinking. Living in the present moment is important because anxiety lives solely in the future. In this moment—the here and now—you are safe and secure. All that you fear are things that aren't real yet and may never be real at all.

SUBTYPES OF TYPE SIX

The following subtypes of type six are based on the three instinctual variants and how those interact with the type six's relationship to fear. The self-preservation type six focuses on the need to be protected, so they look to make the needed connections to be safe. The social type six focuses on the fear of doing the wrong thing in the eyes of authorities and, therefore, looks for rules and guidelines to follow. The sexual type six focuses on denying fear and facing it head-on through a position of strength.

SELF-PRESERVATION
- The most phobic subtype
- Relationship-oriented
- Craves outside support
- Warm and friendly

- Fears disappointing others
- Has a difficult time making decisions
- Carries a lot of blame and guilt
- Can look like a type two

SOCIAL

- Finds comfort in relying on authority
- Focused on understanding and fulfilling his or her role
- In constant pursuit of understanding the rules and expectations
- Believes that everything will go wrong so focuses on doing the right thing
- Can become a fanatic for his or her belief system
- Legalistic
- Punctual, precise, and responsible
- Can look like a type one or three

SEXUAL

- Turns against fear and leans into strength
- When feeling fear, leans into it and runs toward it
- Bold and fierce
- Often focused on being physically strong
- Takes on an intimidating stance
- Has a need to be contrarian and focuses on being the opposite of the group
- Often likes to disrupt and stir up trouble
- Can look like a type eight

TYPE SIX AND WINGS

As a type six, you can pull from either of your wings to help round out your personality. You may find that you already lean in one direction more than the other. However, you have access to the skills and vices of both wings. Here are some qualities you can borrow from your neighbors:

TYPE FIVE WING

When pulling in this wing, you may find yourself tapping into your intellectual and analytical side. You can use this to aid in problem-solving, independence, and the desire to be informed.

TYPE SEVEN WING

This wing can aid you in bringing in a lightness, humor about life, and enhanced energy. Lean into this wing for connecting with others and finding the bright side of potential scenarios.

TYPE SIX AND LINES

When in stress, the type six moves to type three, and when in rest, they move to type nine. With that understanding, here's what you may want to keep in mind in your relationship to stress and self-care.

RECOGNIZING YOUR STRESS

When stressed out, type sixes may find themselves at the lower side of type three. This can look like becoming increasingly image-conscious—attempting to adopt an image that aids you in fitting in with your community or chosen authority. It can look like becoming increasingly competitive and potentially self-promoting, and in extreme scenarios, being dishonest about your background and qualifications, often in pursuit of securing yourself in a comfortable financial or social position.

SELF-CARE INFUSION

When you start to notice this come up in you, you have the tools you need to care for yourself. Using the high side of type nine, you can deeply prioritize your own peace of mind. Take time to rest and participate in nourishing activities. Participate in meditating on the present moment.

RECOGNIZING STAGNATION

In the same way that you can use the peaceful and calming qualities of type nine to relieve stress, you can also end up at the low end of type nine accidentally. This can look like merging to match the group that you are aligned with, settling for less than you truly desire, and losing drive for seeking more from life. It can also manifest through passive-aggressive behavior in attempts to get your needs met.

MOTIVATION INFUSION

This is where it's helpful to bring in the high side of type three. Take your life into your hands and focus on the goals you have for yourself. Taking time to focus on your goals and a higher path of achievement can take your mind off of what you fear and instead focus on what you would like to achieve. You can counter your tendency to undersell yourself and intentionally seek out the recognition that you deserve for your dedication and hard work.

LEVELS OF HEALTH

HEALTHY

In their healthiest state, type sixes release the desire to find support in someone else and learn to listen to their own inner guidance. Healthy type sixes are disciplined, practical, and dependable. The safety and security you crave is found here in your trust of your own inner authority.

AVERAGE

In most cases, our type sixes hold a contradiction inside of them—both a desire for independence and a deep craving for authority and guidance. They seek out procedures, rules, and philosophies by which they can live their lives while also questioning the validity of each one.

UNHEALTHY

The type six may find themselves reactive, panicky, depressed, and feeling helpless. They may harbor paranoid fears and delusional ideas about the world, often becoming obsessive about their fears or imagined enemies.

GETTING H.O.N.E.S.T. FOR TYPE SIX

What I believe is remarkable about type sixes is the deep awareness they bring to the table. I believe type sixes are highly underutilized in relationships and organizations and one of our most untapped resources. The ability to sort out what could be a potential threat helps us to prepare and plan for all possible scenarios. In addition, once you have a type six on your team, you have someone who will go to bat for you as if they are going to bat for themselves—a loyal and supportive friend/teammate who only has your best interests at heart.

What is equally heartbreaking for me is that all of this awareness, this dedication, and this fire gets used mostly for the sake of other people or higher organizations. There's a lack of focus on who you are and what you truly want—not necessarily a lack of "thinking" about these things but more a lack of trust and action around who you are and what you desire. It can seem much easier to focus on what you don't know over what you desire. I beam when I engage with a type six who has found their power—one who has learned to own their inner authority and stand in the truth of who they are and what actually serves them, not just the organizations they belong to.

HONOR YOUR STRENGTHS

The first step is to take time to get really honest with yourself about what makes you amazing. Celebrate all of the elements of your personality that you love. If it's tricky for you to think of things you love about yourself, consider what you do and who you are that contributes positively to the world around you.

A few things that are amazing about type sixes:
- You are considerate.
- You are loyal.
- You are capable and competent.
- You are courageous.
- You stand up for others.
- You are great at reading people.
- You are hardworking and dedicated.
- You take time to do things the right way.
- You have integrity.
- You are great in a crisis.

It's important that you know the goal isn't to avoid being a type six. You don't need to reject everything that you are—even your strengths. It's simply about holding the awareness for what is keeping you away from your essence. It's OK that your good qualities are part of your type pattern—it doesn't make them less good.

Take some time to write out your personal strengths below.

_____

_____

_____

OPEN YOUR EYES TO BLIND SPOTS

This is the section where we run through all of the things that you will want to hold space for while you grow—the things that are habitual but aren't truly serving you in the pursuit of a life where you get to fully express your truest essence. In this, I want to let you know that a couple of these are going to be in direct contradiction to how you've traditionally viewed the world. It may, quite frankly, piss you off. But know that I write these things in love and that I didn't make them up. (They're integrated ancient Enneagram teachings.) You are in the driver's seat of your growth journey—at the end of the day, you decide how much of this is right for you.

For type sixes, it can often feel unsettling to explore releasing your current worldview. It can feel like you're giving up all of the things that bring you comfort and security. However, the reality is that these are things that serve as a Band-Aid for your doubt. They temporarily keep you satisfied until the doubt and fear creep back in again. Working through these can take you to the place where doubt is no longer something to be solved through questioning, testing, and worry, rather just something to move through until it dissipates.

A few things to keep in mind as a type six:

1. Anxiety does not live in the present moment.
Our anxieties exist as an attempt to see the future—a belief that if we try hard enough, we can finally predict what is going to go wrong down the road. While at times this can be a useful skill, it's important to recognize when we are using this for our benefit and when it has taken over and is instead ruling us.

There's a phrase that I think is particularly helpful for us to keep in mind: when we worry, we live through the hard things twice. The experience of stressing over potential trauma can often sit in our bodies as if the trauma were real. Therefore, when we focus our attention on what could go wrong, we live through the experience whether or not we end up having to actually live through it.

Here's the other thing you should know: you are equipped and ready for the crisis when it happens. Think back to every actual hard thing you've ever gone through. You were equipped! I imagine you were calm and competent as well. That's because you have what you need when the actual crisis arises. It's not because you worried about it enough beforehand to make it through. It's because you have instincts and skill sets that equip you for the challenges you face in life.

Be cautious of using anxiety as a false sense of preparation. Instead, recognize it for what it is—purposefully sending yourself through traumatic situations that you may not ever face otherwise.

2. Allow kindness in.
Be cautious of running kind actions and loving words through a bullshit detector. When we approach people who want to share love with us as if they are simply seeking something for themselves, we miss out on integrating the kindness into the understanding of who we are.

Not every kind word or thoughtful action has a plan behind it. Sometimes people just want to share what they like about you or find joy in giving. I encourage you to accept every compliment. That doesn't mean that that person has to become your new best friend, but maybe they saw something in you worth celebrating, and you should celebrate it too.

3. Focusing on potential problems creates real problems.

When we spend our energy focused on what could go wrong, we find that it can often create the exact scenario that we are fearful of. You find yourself focused on a fear that your business is going to fail, so you don't take the necessary risks to grow, and it ends up failing. You fear that someone is unhappy with you, so you act strange and defensive around them, creating an environment where they are more inclined to be unhappy with you. You fear losing your job, so you become increasingly paranoid, competitive, and self-promoting, which creates an uncomfortable and unhealthy work environment when you are around and distracts you from focusing on tasks at hand.

What we focus on is where our energy goes.

4. You are not the group you're aligned with.

While it can be comforting to align yourself with a specific set of ideals, guidelines, and expectations, it's important to remember that your identity is not held within that container. You have desires, needs, passions, and interests outside of your immediate community. This is important to remember when you are seeking counsel outside of yourself or choosing paths for your life or when moments of doubt and insecurity arise.

There is an inherent insecurity in aligning our purpose and identity with something outside of who we are. There's a reliance on what belonging to that group offers you.

With that approach, you are more likely to find yourself struggling to regroup when friendships fall through—more dependent on your relationships and less able to bounce back when you receive negative feedback from a member of your community.

You are worthy, wonderful, and secure just as you are and just where you are. That isn't going anywhere. Learning to lean into that will create a new depth to what true safety really is.

5. Be cautious of "othering" people.
In the pursuit of belonging, we can often find ourselves with a heightened awareness to what doesn't align with our worldview—what belief systems, traditions, and ways of being aren't "like you." This creates a dynamic of seeing people as inherently different from you and, therefore, not as valid or worthy—and sometimes even threatening.

In reality we are all simply trying the best we can with what we've been given. We choose different belief systems, groups to align with, and ways of walking through the world from our own place of deep need. Learning to see ourselves as not separate from other people but instead as all part of the same human experience not only aids us in being people who hold space for world peace but also can bring in a dependent sense of safety while walking through the world.

NOTE YOUR SUPPORT PLAN
This is the part of the process where we get to talk about finding what actually serves YOU when it comes to creating a life that you love. This is very exciting for me to share with type sixes because so often type sixes may have great answers and resources for the other people in their lives but struggle to listen to their own inner knowing when making decisions for themselves.

So, how do we learn to listen to our own inner authority and trust that we have what we need to be safe? For our type sixes, I encourage you to do something very out of the ordinary. I want you to run your fear all the way to its worst-case scenario. Out loud. What are you truly afraid of? It's often not the worst-case scenario but the idea of not knowing.

Below, you will find a list of things that may support you in the process of building self-trust, relieving anxiety, living in the present moment, and opening yourself to oneness.

A few things that may support you in the process:

- Create a decision-making process for yourself. I enjoy a nice pro/con list, but you can also brain-dump all of your fears or worries onto paper as a way to clear out your mind.
- Let your fear run its course. This sounds counterintuitive, but by giving voice to our concerns and letting them out to the most extreme point, we give them their time in the sun while also exposing how extreme and unrealistic our concerns truly are.
- Practice loving-kindness meditations. These mediations focus on experience empathy for other people. Take time to meditate on those whose world views are in direct opposition to your own.
- Periodically check in to the present moment. What do you see, smell, hear, taste, and touch that brings you joy right here and right now?
- Limit your feedback panel to one or two people who have a clear understanding of what you want for your life.
- Take yourself out on adventures. Set a budget and a time frame that feels comfortable to you, and make no other decisions until you leave to go out. Take each move as it comes—not preparing or planning—just exercising the joy in spontaneity.
- Find a community centered around movement that you enjoy—a Zumba class, yoga, cycling, dance, etc.—something that you can share with others that takes you out of day-to-day life and gets you into your body.
- Get into things and communities that aren't the one you're most comfortable with. Experience the joy in a diverse social network and create a foundation of stability outside of one small community of people.

What can you do this week to contribute to your self-trust and presence?

EXPLORE YOUR RELATIONSHIPS

So far, you've honored your strengths, gotten really honest with yourself about your blind spots, and set aside a plan of support in the process. Now it's time to talk about relationships. It's all well and good to do all of this work on our own, but what do we do when someone else comes in and they disrupt our perfect synchronicity of self-compassion? This is where we get to explore what you bring into your relationships. What do you positively contribute? What do you do that doesn't serve your work to being the brave, loving, and independent person that you are in your essence?

Beautiful things that type sixes bring to their relationships:
- Showing up for those you love.
- Consistency.
- Doing anything for those you care about.
- Having the best interests of those you love at heart.
- Keeping up with people—not often losing touch.
- Helping people think through the decisions they're going to make.

A few things that may not be serving your relationships:
- Using your friends as sounding boards for every decision you make.
- Being consumed with worry and skepticism to the point of taking you out of the experience you're sharing together.
- Projecting your fears onto the people in your life and people you don't know.
- Merging to match the tone of the group.
- Being unnecessarily contrarian, pulling your energy down as a way to balance out a happy group or raising your energy high as a way to balance out a sad situation.

- Being more loyal to others than they are to you; it's important for you to learn when to release friendships that aren't serving you.

The reason we're talking about this—even if it's uncomfortable and sometimes painful—is because, in the long run it will bring you so much relief. Holding the truth that both of these lists exist simultaneously is the key to ease in your relationships. Knowing what you can control and what isn't yours to worry about can be an extremely relaxing move to make. That tiny list up there, that's it. Think about that! You are doing so much right!

Take a few minutes to think of your own lists. Write down what you personally bring to your relationships, both positively and negatively!

Now, take a few moments here to think of the three most important relationships in your life. Write out how you would like for them to feel. How would they change if you could imagine a world where they were exactly as you hoped?

What about your lists would need to shift in order to have the relationships that you want?

SOFTEN YOUR PATH

OK, so we've established what makes you amazing. (Way to go, by the way!) We've covered what areas of your life may be in need of some tender love and care. We've even discussed how to support yourself in this growth. Let's now talk about how we're going to keep this process going even when it feels difficult or impossible or a bit too unnatural.

I want to give you these three soft internal shifts to make—just three things to hold on to each and every day that will help you in the work of being your healthiest type six self.

1. Focus on the present moment.
If you take nothing else away from this chapter, I hope that you take away the reality that in this moment, you are fine. You are breathing and able to think through what you're feeling. If you have time to worry, you must not have anything really to worry about. If a true crisis were here, you would turn that piece of your brain off and you'd take care of the situation. With that in mind, take time to sit and acknowledge what is here in this moment. What is present? This will allow you to get out of your head and into the reality of your life.

2. Filter circumstances, not people.
It's common for type sixes to filter people through the lens of being trustworthy or untrustworthy. This often happens within the first five seconds of meeting someone. I encourage you to spend less energy attempting to prevent someone from getting too close to you and instead focusing on each interaction. Be honest about which circumstances work for you and which don't. Express boundaries clearly and allow yourself to exit a situation that isn't working for you.

This works in reverse as well. For a lot of type sixes, once someone has made it through your filter, you don't see a world without them in it. This can lead you to staying in relationships, friendships, and situations that, at best, aren't working for you anymore and, at worst, are unhealthy.

3. Exercise your independence muscle.
Get cozy doing things on your own. Take yourself out, make decisions without feedback from others, and go out and do something that requires you to meet new people without any of your friends or family with you. Practice the feeling of stability that comes with having a deep and trusting relationship to who you are without your support system.

TURN THAT INTO SOMETHING BEAUTIFUL

Creativity is important for all types. But I think it's particularly important for type sixes to have somewhere to expend all of their mental energy as well as having a thing that is only for you.

So, what do you, as a type six, need to keep in mind when it comes to creativity?

- There is no wrong way to be creative. Just have fun with it!
- You can try something and change your mind and try something else. This is the best place for you to explore releasing things that aren't working for you any longer.
- Definitely be creative with friends if you'd like to be. But also make sure that it's not limited to only when you are with people. Enjoy creating things just for you as well.
- You don't have to follow the path of someone else. Get a little weird with it and mix things up. Tap into a part of yourself that is willing to break rules, get messy, and try something different.
- Try out intuitive painting. Grab a blank canvas and just see what your next stroke will be. This is a fun and playful way for you to tap into asking yourself questions and trusting your inner guidance.
- Be cautious of ignoring this part of yourself altogether. It can be a bit too easy for a lot of type sixes to pretend they aren't creative in nature and to ignore that part of who they are. By ignoring this, you are missing out on a very rich element of being human that can bring in the lightness, independence, and peace that is available to you.

Dear Six

I'm enthralled with the way you show up for the people in your life. Your consistency, loyalty, and awareness are so inspiring to me.

I want you to know that you are brave.

I also want you to know that you deserve rest. You deserve time where you aren't living your life through the lens of what could go wrong. I want you to have time where your focus of attention is simply on what is real and right in the here and now.

Life will come as it does. No amount of thinking, worrying, or preparation will prevent it from coming to fruition. So while I know it can be tempting to guard us all from the pain of life, you can rest now. When the problems arise, we can deal with them together.

In the meantime, I hope that you know you're strong and capable and really thorough. You can trust yourself. You can take the time you need to treat yourself and chase the desires of your heart.

I think of type sixes kind of like superheroes-in-waiting—people who are so powerful even though there is no imminent threat. When the threat arises, you're so capable and ready. But where do you put all of that energy while you're waiting? You've trained your whole life for the threat, so those muscles are in overdrive in the in-between. It's time for you to give yourself something to focus on other than waiting for the next bad thing to happen. Get busy with hobbies, movement practices, and meditation. Entertain yourself and play with life—you deserve it!

ENTHUSIAST

MULTI-TASKER

WUNDERKIND

ILLUMINATOR
OF POSSIBLITY

*"I know that I will be OK as long as
I get my needs met."*

All the things!	"I'm really into ___ right now."	Alone in public.	Buys plane ticket, figures the rest out later	FOMO.
"It'll work out."	Saves tears for when they're alone in the car	Rose-colored glasses.	"I can't wait for . . ."	1,001 hobbies.
Lots of small plates.	Has strong opinion—changes mind the next day	7	Fears commitment	Savory and sweet combo.
Tells jokes when comforting someone	Plays the game "How Many Things Can I Get Done in 5 Minutes?"	Positive vibes only.	Optimistic AF.	"Come on . . . Let's just do it."
Resents expectations	Loves everyone—needs no one	Already works on new things before the last thing is finished	Bucket lists.	"I think one day I'd really like to . . ."

PRIVATE MOMENTS

By Enneagram type.

1 - TURNING ALL OF THE BATHROOM PRODUCT LABELS IN THE SAME DIRECTION.

2 - WRITING A LETTER TO THEIR FUTURE SPOUSE.

3 - PRACTICING THEIR ACCEPTANCE SPEECH.

4 - PRETENDING THEY'RE IN A MOVIE.

5 - REMEMBERING EXACTLY WHAT SOMEONE WAS WEARING ON JUNE 21, 2018.

6 - PLANNING OUT WHAT THEY WOULD DO TO HANDLE DIFFERENT SCENARIOS THAT MAY COME UP.

7 - PLAYING THE "HOW MANY RIDICULOUS FACES CAN I MAKE IN 30 SECONDS" GAME WHEN THEY'RE AT A STOPLIGHT.

8 - DOING THINGS THE HARDER WAY JUST TO PROVE TO THEMSELVES THAT THEY CAN.

9 - REHEARSING ALL OF THE COMEBACKS THAT THEY "SHOULD" HAVE SAID EARLIER.

@enneagramandcoffee

ABOUT TYPE SEVEN

Basic Desire: "It's important to me that I remain happy, satisfied, and fulfilled."

Basic Fear: "I am most afraid of being deprived and trapped in negative emotions."

Type sevens are cheerful, fun-loving, and adventurous. In childhood, type sevens often lost faith in the potential for them to find adequate nurturing. Through this process, they learned to nurture themselves through staying entertained and choosing positive emotions. While there is a nice side to being able to care for yourself, it is often what creates a cycle of excessive indulgence for the type seven. Type sevens spend a lot of their time focused on the next great experience and looking for the next good thing to keep them occupied and entertained. Type sevens are curious, bold, fast learners, joyful, and often somewhat of a renaissance person.

I titled type sevens "Illuminators of Possibility" because they have the tendency to focus on the positive potential of the future. Through this, they experience so much richness in life. They take risks and refuse to accept limitations of any kind. Through this, they are often able to live in such a way that is inspiring to those around them who often give themselves less permission. They are also quick to be the first person to tell you all the ways in which your idea could and will work out!

Most type sevens live with an underlying vibration of anxiety—something lingering in the back of their minds that serves as something of an internal motor. This motor pushes them to keep busy and moving so that they don't have to be fully present with the painful emotions that arise as part of being human. Type sevens have the tendency to ignore, deny, or fight the reality of anger, sadness, fear, disappointment, and other negative emotions. They fight this through staying constantly entertained and reframing the experience into a positive. For many type sevens, negative emotions can feel like quicksand. If you dip your toes into the darkness, there's a fear that you won't get back out—that it will consume you, sinking further and further until you can't get out. It's mostly unconscious, of course, but it causes the type seven to overbook so that they don't have to be alone with their thoughts. When they are face-to-face with their negative emotions, it's often very easy for a type seven to turn those into something that in another light is actually a good thing. A lot of the work for our type sevens comes down to learning how to access the other half of their emotions and be willing to sit with and acknowledge their sadness, anger, and fear. This will free them up not to be dependent upon their coping mechanisms, which can often cause them to give up quickly on relationships, careers, and other interests that, after a while, end up having their own sort of discomfort.

SUBTYPES OF TYPE SEVEN

The following subtypes of type seven are based on the three instinctual variants and how those interact with the type seven's relationship to excessive indulgence. The self-preservation type seven indulges in satisfying opportunities and forming a network of allies. The social type seven focuses on a counter-indulgence through serving other people. The sexual type seven indulges through amazing experiences and seeking the ultimate relationship.

SELF-PRESERVATION
- The most practical and concrete of the subtypes
- Tends to form a "family" or group of allies as a support group
- Great networkers
- Opportunistic
- Hedonistic
- Talkative and friendly
- Grounded and earthy
- Can seem like a type six or eight

SOCIAL
- Dedicated
- Anti-indulgent
- Fears being excessive
- Makes it a virtue to get by on less
- Takes on a lot of responsibility
- Has a deep need for admiration
- Always exists for the sake of other people
- Often confused that they feel both altruistic and self-interested
- Can seem like a type one or two

SEXUAL
- The most ethereal of the subtypes
- A large focus on everything being OK
- Imaginative
- Idealistic
- Wants to try everything
- Naive
- Rose-colored glasses
- Trusting and hopeful
- Spends more time imagining than doing

TYPE SEVEN AND WINGS

As a type seven, you can pull from either of your wings to help round out your personality. You may find that you already lean in one direction more than the other. However, you have access to the skills and vices of both wings. Here are some qualities you can borrow from your neighbors:

TYPE SIX WING

Use this wing to help you think things through before leaping. It can help you put systems in place that support your career. It's great for aiding you in being more connected and consistent in your relationships.

TYPE EIGHT WING

This wing can help you accomplish your goals, ask for what you need, and become more strategic about where you place your energy. Through this wing, you can deepen your relationship to pleasure as well as find your source of power.

TYPE SEVEN AND LINES

When in stress, the type seven moves to type one, and when in rest, they move to type five. With that understanding, here's what you may want to keep in mind in your relationship to stress and self-care:

RECOGNIZING YOUR STRESS

When stressed out, type sevens find themselves at the lower side of type one. In this mode, you may find that you are becoming overly strict with yourself and others, placing high expectations for what you can produce and what you expect from people in your life. This process can either cause you to rebel against your own expectations, becoming even more scattered and flaky, or you may find yourself becoming more and more rigid and serious, losing the light, happy nature you're used to.

SELF-CARE INFUSION

When you start to notice this come up in you, you have the tools you need to care for yourself. Using the high side of type five, you can swap discipline for strategy. Focus on your top priorities, deepen your knowledge on a single topic, and enjoy time alone with your thoughts. Learning not to fill your time with constant entertainment will give you the depth of self-care that you need in order to move through stress with more ease.

RECOGNIZING STAGNATION

In the same way that you can use the self-sufficient and informed aspects of type five, you can also accidentally slip into the lower side of that type. This can look like flaking on responsibilities, cutting people out of your life when they bring negative emotions into your space, and getting lost in your thoughts. In the same way that type fives can escape into fantasy, type sevens can get carried away in daydreaming about future joy instead of dealing with today's reality.

MOTIVATION INFUSION

This is where it's helpful to bring in the high side of type one. Enlist a strong sense of right and wrong to run your decisions through. It can also be incredibly helpful to create structure and discipline for yourself to put action to all of your great ideas!

LEVELS OF HEALTH

HEALTHY

In their healthiest state, type sevens quit looking for things outside of themselves to make them happy. They live in the moment, fully living out their experiences. They live in a state of gratitude and possibility. They are optimistic and vivacious but also put action to their ideas and see them to fruition.

AVERAGE

In most cases, our type sevens are afraid of missing out. They can be restless and focused on maintaining variety and limiting restriction. They can be very busy, often having every second of their day scheduled out or even double-booked. There's a constant pursuit of being entertained, and more isn't enough. They can feel hard to please and left always wanting more.

UNHEALTHY

The type seven may find that they become impulsive and irresponsible, seeking anything that will provide temporary relief from their negative emotions. Their seeking for "more" can lead to addictions, financial ruin, and sabotaged relationships.

GETTING H.O.N.E.S.T. FOR TYPE SEVEN

What I believe is remarkable about type seven is ultimately their resilience—the deep ability to take the worst that life has to offer and not only keep going but keep going with a smile on their face. Type sevens are like living sunshine, breathing life and joy into any room that they walk into. Type sevens take life as a challenge—to make the absolute most out of the time we are given, do everything their heart aches to do, and chase every dream no matter how small. For this reason, type sevens can be incredibly inspirational to those who carry more fear by nature. Finally, type sevens are very quick learners and are often naturally skilled at new things. This can mean that a lot of type sevens develop a wide range of skills and experience over the course of their lives.

What is equally heartbreaking for me is that all of the magic that is locked inside of our type sevens can be lost in the desperate attempt to escape the full experience of life. With all of the desire not to be limited, type sevens are often their own greatest limiters—keeping themselves limited emotionally, financially, and relationally through their compulsive need to avoid pain.

HONOR YOUR STRENGTHS

The first step is to take time to get really honest with yourself about what makes you amazing. Celebrate all of the elements of your personality that you love. If it's tricky for you to think of things you love about yourself, consider what you do and who you are that contributes positively to the world around you.

A few things that are amazing about type sevens:
- You are sunshine.
- You are expansive.
- You are a quick learner.
- You are bold.
- You bring light to the lives of others.
- You are adventurous
- You are full of amazing ideas.
- You are resilient.
- You are grateful.

- You are engaging, bright, and lively.
- You are great at anything you put your mind to.
- You are a living example of a life well lived.

It's important that you know the goal isn't to not be a type seven. You don't need to reject everything that you are—even your strengths. It's simply about holding the awareness for what is keeping you away from your essence. It's OK that your good qualities are part of your type pattern—it doesn't make them less good.

Take some time to write out your personal strengths below.

_____

_____

_____

_____

_____

OPEN YOUR EYES TO BLIND SPOTS

This is the section where we run through all of the things that you will want to hold space for while you grow—the things that are habitual but aren't truly serving you in the pursuit of a life where you get to fully express your truest essence. In this, I want to let you know that a couple of these are going to be in direct contradiction to how you've traditionally viewed the world. It may, quite frankly, piss you off. But know that I write these things in love, and that I didn't make them up. (They're integrated ancient Enneagram teachings.) You are in the driver's seat of your growth journey—at the end of the day you decide how much of this is right for you.

For type sevens, it is particularly important that we sit with these things. It can be easy for type sevens to dismiss their blind spots and vices and reframe their guilt into a more digestible emotion. But you are stronger than that. So we're going to talk really honestly about the blind spots of type sevens so that we can move through them, doing less harm to ourselves and others.

A few things to keep in mind as a type seven:

1. You cannot outrun your responsibilities.
In this moment, where you are pursuing the next great thing, take time to ask yourself what it is you're leaving behind? Have you set out a budget? Are you ignoring your bank account? Are there people who are relying on you? Have you properly quit your job?

You can't ignore the responsibilities of life forever. It can seem like you can outrun them, and if you keep moving, they won't catch up with you—leaving a stream of unpaid parking tickets, cancelled plans, and deferred student loans. At some point, you will have to take care of all of this.

Here's the secret: it is so much easier to do right in the moment as soon as it arises—take care of your obligations before you're tempted to spend the money on a plane ticket or a nice dinner. Just take care of it before it all piles up and becomes one big neglected responsibility monster that lives on your shoulder, making you crave more and more distractions.

2. There is no end to wanting "more."
When you build your life's satisfaction around the idea of doing things that make you happy, buying things to cheer yourself up, or entertaining yourself with food and beverage, there is no true satisfaction that can be achieved. This leaves you in constant pursuit of whatever the next good thing will be.

The work here is learning to find satisfaction in needing less, in simply existing in the world. The reason this is important is that eventually what used to work for you won't work anymore, and you'll find yourself looking for bigger, more intense distractions to keep you satisfied. Focus your energy on things that truly satisfy so you can create that for yourself without the negative consequences of excessive indulgence.

3. All ideas aren't for you to create.
You are not responsible for bringing to life every single idea that comes to your mind. You aren't missing out on anything if you put that idea in a safe place and let it stay there for a while. Type sevens have so many ideas firing off in their minds at all times. It can be tempting to put your energy into pursuing each of those individually. What happens when you do this is that you find yourself scattered, confused, and getting nowhere. Building ten bridges to the same island all at once will get you nowhere, but focusing all of your energy on one bridge will get you all the way.

This doesn't mean that you'll never try these ideas. I just recommend writing them down somewhere safe, and when the time is right, you can revisit the list. Give your projects time to be successful, or you will struggle for the rest of your life.

4. It doesn't matter how good your story is; if you haven't expressed interest in their thoughts, they don't want to hear it.
Type sevens spend a lot of time doing things, thinking about those things, and engaging with people. This can create a buildup of untold stories. Interesting experiences, thoughts, or conversations can crowd your mind, waiting for the right time to be told. However, sometimes these stories get shared in lieu of true connection with other people. Conversations can feel like story time, leaving those engaging with

you feeling like they received a good performance but not so much a great interaction.

Be intentional to ask questions of those with whom you're speaking. Pique your natural curiosity about who they are, and play with not sharing about yourself without being directly asked to. Enjoy the feeling of being curious about the internal world of another person.

5. Living in the future is limiting the fullness you are experiencing in life.
It's common for type sevens to find the most joy in preparation—the thoughts of their next big thing or their next exciting opportunity, and spending hours daydreaming, planning, and preparing for the next time they know they'll experience joy.

As a type seven myself, I'll never forget the moment I stood in front of the Eiffel Tower for the first time. I had a six-month road trip planned for when I got home. I looked at the tower, and I looked at my travel partner and said, "I can't wait for the road trip." Their response to me was something along the lines of, "Are you insane right now? You're standing in front of the Eiffel Tower talking about being somewhere else."

That's the trap we can set for ourselves as type sevens. When we build so much of our joy on the anticipation of the moment, once we get there we're not quite satisfied with it. We're already done with it and moved on to the next thing, leaving us craving more and more stimulation.

NOTE YOUR SUPPORT PLAN
This is the part of the process where we get to talk about finding what actually serves YOU when it comes to creating a life that you love.

This is very exciting for me to share with type sevens because so often type sevens have so much energy for possibility but lose steam in the process of making possibility into a reality.

So, how do we learn to listen to live in the beauty of now and allow for both the positive and negative to exist in our lives? For our type sevens, I encourage you to sit in silence for one minute. Place your hand on your heart, your stomach, or your lap. Breathe in and ask yourself what is real for you right now? What feelings are you afraid of experiencing?

Below, you will find a list of things that may support you in the process of building the ability to sit with your feelings, dedication to following through, and satisfaction with the present moment.

A few things that may support you in the process:
- Keep an idea journal. Write down all of the ideas that come to you, so you don't forget them but you don't have to act on them immediately.
- Practice meditation and intentional breathing as a way to sit with what is arising for you emotionally.
- Develop a habit of checking in with your responsibilities once a day or once a week in a way that feels good to you. A weekly date with your finances will do wonders!
- Write three pages of free thought every morning. Get all of your thoughts, fears, ideas, and anxieties out of your head first thing every day so that you can focus on what you want to accomplish.
- Set reverse deadlines for yourself—such as an amount of time that you promise to stick with something before quitting. This will help you make a conscious decision to move on from something versus an impulsive act of avoidance that could easily be regretted later.

- Keep a note of small joys throughout your day—simple things that didn't cost you money or extra time that make you smile. This will help you tap into your essence of full satisfaction and gratitude from right where you are.
- Practice staying home alone. It will be hard at first, but eventually, the more comfortable you are with time by yourself in your house, the easier it will be for you not to fill your time with things that aren't serving you.
- Make it a habit to regularly volunteer your time to those in need. Get out of your normal mode of thinking and focus on the needs of others.

What can you do this week to contribute to your life?

EXPLORE YOUR RELATIONSHIPS

So far, you've honored your strengths, gotten really honest with yourself about your blind spots, and set aside a plan of support in the process. Now it's time to talk about relationships. It's all well and good to do all of this work on our own, but what do we do when someone else comes in and they disrupt our perfect synchronicity of self-compassion? This is where we get to explore what you bring into your relationships. What do you positively contribute? What do you do that doesn't serve your work to being the brave, loving, and independent person that you are in your essence?

Beautiful things that type sevens bring to their relationships:
- Bringing joy to every day.
- Curating really amazing experiences for people in your life.
- Encouraging people to be more of who they want to be in the world.
- Showing us how not to take things so seriously.

- Being fun to be around.
- Helping people take the needed risks to follow their hearts' desires.

A few things that may not be serving your relationships:
- Ignoring the difficult parts of relationship in favor of the next fun thing.
- Neglecting your responsibilities often, leaving them for someone else to do.
- Bailing on plans for something that seemed more exciting.
- Not being willing to sit and listen to others describe the harder parts of life.
- Being overly critical of those who stand in the way of you avoiding negative emotion.
- Prioritizing your needs over the needs of others.

The reason we're talking about this—even if it's uncomfortable and sometimes painful—is because in the long run it will bring you so much relief. Holding the truth that both of these lists exist simultaneously is the key to ease in your relationships. Knowing what you can control and what isn't yours to worry about can be an extremely relaxing move to make. That tiny list up there, that's it. Think about that! You are doing so much right!

Take a few minutes to think of your own lists. Write down what you personally bring to your relationships, both positively and negatively.

Now, take a few moments here to think of the three most important relationships in your life. Write out how you would like for them to feel. How would they change if you could imagine a world where they were exactly as you hoped?

What about your lists would need to shift in order to have the relationships that you want?

SOFTEN YOUR PATH

OK, so we've established what makes you amazing. (Way to go, by the way!) We've covered what areas of your life may be in need of some tender love and care. We've even discussed how to support yourself in this growth. Let's now talk about how we're going to keep this process going, even when it feels difficult or impossible or a bit too unnatural.

I want to give you these four soft internal shifts to make—just four things to hold on to each and every day that will help you in the work of being your healthiest type seven self.

1. Learn to sit with darkness through breathing.
Find a pattern of breathing and connecting to your body that will allow you to sit with difficult emotions. This can be immensely helpful not only for dealing with your own emotions but also for sitting with the negative emotions of others or in relational conflict.

2. Set reverse deadlines.
Set time frames for yourself to stick to the things you want to try. This will help you not to prematurely end a career, hobby, relationship, or other experience. Sit through the discomfort for the amount of time you promised yourself, and then—and only then—decide if you will continue on with it or let it go.

3. Exercise your gratitude muscle.
In your essence, you are satisfied with the ordinariness of life. Every piece of existence is spectacular to you. However, in average states of health, it is more common for you to need an extraordinary experi-

ence. Experiences that are fleeting in satisfaction ultimately just leave you wanting for something more.

Make a point to write down what you are grateful for in everyday life. Keep a list of good things you see throughout your day as a way to stay present with what is good in the here and now.

4. Date your responsibilities.
Find a regular time that you check in with the responsibilities of life—a weekly date to pay bills, water the plants, check the oil in your car, etc. Make this fun if you'd like to (although be cautious of making it expensive or excessively indulgent). Indulge lightly in a nice cup of coffee or a beautiful location and do the hard stuff!

TURN THAT INTO SOMETHING BEAUTIFUL
Creativity is important for all types. But having a creative outlet is almost not even a choice for most type sevens. Their minds are reeling with ideas and concepts that they want to try. The work for most type sevens is in following through with that desire.

So, what do you as a type seven need to keep in mind when it comes to creativity?
- Just because you want to do it doesn't mean it has to happen right this moment.
- Change up your location when you find yourself losing focus.
- Try the Pomodoro Technique for enhancing your productivity: focus for twenty minutes, take a five-minute break, focus for another twenty minutes, etc.
- Keep a weekly to-do list instead of a daily one, then focus on just three tasks that you intend to accomplish each day. This will help you to prioritize your energy and focus on the things that really matter.

- Do a public creativity experiment as a form of accountability. Write for thirty days straight and let people follow along, do a self-portrait series, paint something new each week for a year, or any other thing that keeps you focused on following through with what you want to make.
- Be cautious of filling your time up so much that you never get bored enough to come up with original ideas. Great thoughts and concepts arise when you have time to breathe. Making something incredible can't happen in the moments between driving from one event to another event. You need space and time and the ability to get nice and bored.

Dear Seven

We both know that you are so much more than fun. You are rich with depth and interest that many don't really understand.

What I love about you is that you are alive. You are living this life from a place of passion and light that many may never get to experience. Through living such a joyful, experienced, and interesting existence, you subtly give others the permission to do the same, and that's incredible.

If you take nothing else away from this chapter, I hope that you can hold on to the realization that when you feel the desire to flee, when you have that itch arise that makes you want to run away and change your name and start all over again, you may simply be trying not to feel something that's ultimately a very simple feeling.

The idea that our feelings are quicksand is one to be aware of. The fear that you will be sucked in and not have a way out can be so sub-conscious that you may not realize your actions have formed in direct relation to that feeling. Take time to honor your negative emotions, and you'll find that you move through them with much more ease, and ultimately will need much less stimulation to maintain your naturally joyful spirit!

LEADER

CHALLENGER

PROTECTOR

DEFENDER OF
JUSTICE

Type Eight

"I know that I will be OK as long as I remain strong and powerful."

Provides for people they love	Has been in a fight with a stranger	"Why would that hurt your feelings?"	"I can smell your weakness."	Trusts their gut
"Get out of the way, I've got this."	"You can't worry about what people think of you."	Keeps going until the project is complete	"What are you trying to get out of this?"	Doesn't go to sleep angry
"No, we need to talk about this."	"You can't get mad at the truth."	⑧	Protective of the vulnerable.	Work is life.
"We could do that or we could do what I want to do instead."	Top-notch bullsh*t detector.	"I give zero f*cks what you think of me."	Does things the hard way	"You can't treat people like that!"
"They're wrong."	All-nighters.	"Give that to me, I'll take care of it."	Honesty.	Is called "intimidating"

THINGS YOU COME HOME TO

When you're living with a . . .

1 - MARIE KONDO-ING THE TUPPERWARE DRAWER

2 - PRESENTS

3 - AN UPDATED VISION FOR THE NEXT 6 MONTHS

4 - MUSIC PLAYING AND CANDLES LIT

5 - AN UPDATE ON THE IDEA THEY'VE BEEN RESEARCHING

6 - QUESTIONS

7 - HONESTLY, IT COULD BE ANYTHING!

8 - "I DECIDED TO RE-DO THE KITCHEN CABINETS TODAY!"

9 - A RUNDOWN OF THEIR DAY & ALL OF THE THINGS THEY DIDN'T SAY TO PEOPLE THAT THEY WISH THEY'D SAID.

@enneagramandcoffee

ABOUT TYPE EIGHT

Basic Desire: "It's important to me that I am able to determine my own path in life."

Basic Fear: "I am most afraid of being harmed or controlled by others."

Type eights are strong, charismatic leaders. In childhood, type eights often experienced some form of betrayal—something that settled the idea into them that they would need to take care of themselves. Because of this, they learn to lean on their strength and hide their vulnerabilities to prevent being open and susceptible to further betrayal in the future. This can lead our type eights to develop a constant defensive stance. This can happen both in defense of themselves and of those in need.

Type eights are bold, independent, honest, magnanimous, and likely the person who has continually pushed you to be more thoughtful, egalitarian, and driven in your own life.

I titled type eights "Defenders of Justice" because that's what I believe type eights bring to our society the most. They are the people who won't let us go to sleep on those who are being exploited. For many of the other types, it can feel like "too much" or even too scary to wake up every day and ask more of society. But type eights keep showing up each and every day, bravely navigating the terrain of asking for more from our government, our bosses, and each of us. Without type eights, I don't think we would see the major movements we've seen and will continue to see in furthering human, animal, and environmental rights.

Most type eights live in a constant defensive stance—not out of a place of aggression but rather out of a place of protecting their right to choose for themselves. The loss of control in their life is not an option, and it can feel like it is in constant danger of being lost. Type eights are naturally drawn to positions of power and aren't afraid to take the role of leader. In fact, the fear only comes in at the thought of losing their role as protector or provider.

For many type eights, there's a fervor for the underdog and an intolerance for people who exploit those who are vulnerable. Because of this, you may find that type eights take on the role of defender, protector, and even provider for those who aren't able to do so for themselves. On the flip side, there can be an impatience with those who don't stand up for themselves. Type eights will push others to be direct, honest, and firm with their boundaries.

Type eights value honesty and directness, not often fluffing up statements to make them more palatable to others. I think because of this, our type eights can be extremely misunderstood. I think there's a desire, at times, a cry from the people that our type eights put their fire out to make us all more comfortable. But often this comes from our own fear that we will have to become strong. Type eights softening themselves up and becoming milquetoast is the worst thing I could imagine. Instead, the work is in recognizing when strength is arising as a way to avoid vulnerability, and when it is arising because it's time to be strong.

SUBTYPES OF TYPE EIGHT

The following subtypes of type eight are based on the three instinctual variants and how those interact with the type eight's relationship to power. The self-preservation type eight uses his or her power to survive, the social type eight focuses on protecting others and fighting injustice, and the sexual type eight turns this into a fight against convention.

SELF-PRESERVATION

- Focuses on going for what they want
- Least expressive of the subtypes
- No-nonsense
- Direct
- Productive
- Has a quiet strength
- Can be overtly vengeful
- Can be mistaken for a type one or five

SOCIAL

- Service-minded
- Loyal and friendly
- Aware and protective of people being exploited
- Less quick to anger than the other subtypes
- Can find themselves very busy with projects
- Possesses a blind spot where their own needs for love are concerned
- Can resemble a type two or nine

SEXUAL

- Rebellious
- Emotional
- Contrarian
- Doesn't mind being seen as "bad"
- Seeks power and authority
- Focuses on excessive pleasure in life
- Most intellectual of the subtypes
- Demands loyalty but may not be faithful in return
- Not likely to be mistyped

TYPE EIGHT AND WINGS

As a type eight, you can pull from either of your wings to help round out your personality. You may find that you already lean in one direction more than the other. However, you have access to the skills and vices of both wings. Here are some qualities you can borrow from your neighbors:

TYPE SEVEN WING

Using this wing can aid you in becoming more entrepreneurial, persuasive, and inspiring. This wing can be used to bring lightness to your strength and joy to your process.

TYPE NINE WING

This wing can help you open up to the perspectives of others. It can also aid you in being steadier and less easily agitated. This can also be a great place for you to pull in servant-leadership qualities that will serve you well in life.

TYPE EIGHT AND LINES

When in stress, the type eight moves to type five, and when in rest, they move to type two. With that understanding, here's what you may want to keep in mind in your relationship to stress and self-care.

RECOGNIZING YOUR STRESS

When stressed out, type eights may find themselves retreating into the lower levels of type five and hiding out and isolating themselves from the outside world. They may become increasingly reclusive, secretive, and preoccupied with planning and preparing for future projects. In more extreme cases, the type eight may find that they're starting to feel like they are alone in the world and are fundamentally different and isolated from the rest of humanity.

SELF-CARE INFUSION

When you start to notice this come up in you, you have the tools you need to care for yourself. Using the high side of type two, you can open up to others in a genuine and vulnerable way. This will bring you the connection you need to soften your defenses. In a similar way, you may find it helpful to spend time with children or animals as a touchpoint for accessing your heart center. Type eights have giant hearts that are often fiercely guarded. Children and animals pose little threat to most type eights and can therefore be a safe space to intentionally open up to your vulnerability.

RECOGNIZING STAGNATION

In the same way that you can use the self-sufficient and informed aspects of type two, you can easily slip into the low side of that type accidentally. This can look like replacing true vulnerability with false flattery and people-pleasing tendencies. This can happen in particular when you are giving in order to receive—charming others, flattering them, and being helpful as a replacement for asking directly for what you need.

MOTIVATION INFUSION

This is where it's helpful to bring in the high side of type five. This move can help you find balance in your efforts. You can start to recognize when you need nurturing yourself. Using the five's natural gifts for boundaries and energy management, you can pay attention to when you've overextended yourself personally and professionally. Learn to listen to your body, and set healthy limits on what you commit your time to.

LEVELS OF HEALTH

HEALTHY

In their healthiest state, type eights release the idea that they must maintain control of their environment. They learn to release their defensive stance and connect with others vulnerably and with an open heart. The strength in the healthy type eight is primarily used for the common good—helping, protecting, and providing for others while working to remain open, vulnerable, and compassionate.

AVERAGE

In most cases, our type eights are concerned with having the resources they need to accomplish what they've set out to do. They may become more business-like and competitive while guarding their own vulnerabilities. At this level, type eights may feel the need to prove their position of leadership through boastfulness and big promises. They may become coercive and demanding as a way of getting their needs met.

UNHEALTHY

The type eight may find that they feel constantly betrayed and unable to trust anyone. They become antagonistic and vengeful as a way to preemptively squash threats. They lose respect for boundaries and often overreach while also burning their own candle at both ends.

GETTING H.O.N.E.S.T. FOR TYPE EIGHT

What I believe is remarkable about type eights is their amazing ability to lead us all to incredible places. I honestly find it very relaxing to be in the presence of a type eight. I trust type eights to look out for the group and get things done in the way that is effective, efficient, and beneficial to the whole. In addition, I find the direct communication style of type eights refreshing. I love knowing exactly where I stand with someone. It allows me to know very quickly what you are looking for and if I'm the person to meet that need. In general, I think type eights are grossly underserved in the world of Enneagram. Strong, powerful people aren't always using their powers for evil.

In fact, I believe it's the rare few (in all types) that actually have ill intentions. Most of us are just trying to survive. When we realize that being an type eight means living life in constant awareness of people who may have bad intentions for you, it allows us to see the underlying vulnerability there. In general, though, I just have a whole hell of a lot of respect for type eights. If we all approached the world as directly, confidently, and empowered as our type eights, the world would be a simpler place with more people living out their passions and fewer people being exploited.

What is equally heartbreaking for me is that life constantly on defense is a lonely one—not only feeling the pressure to carry the weight of everything on your shoulders but also feeling like you can't reveal how hard it all is and how scared you may be. It's isolating. So many type eights wake up every day and push themselves well beyond human limits. They stay focused on continued awareness of where they are in the power structure, and they limit the ability of others to see their perceived weakness. When we attempt to hide behind our strength, we miss out on the freedom, connection, and deep love of being fully seen for who we are. We also miss out on the healing power of having our own burdens carried alongside us. You don't have to do this alone.

HONOR YOUR STRENGTHS

The first step is to take time to get really honest with yourself about what makes you amazing. Celebrate all of the elements of your personality that you love. If it's tricky for you to think of things you love about yourself, consider what you do and who you are that contributes positively to the world around you.

A few things that are amazing about type eights:
- You are direct and communicative.
- You are a great leader.
- You are driven and goal-oriented.
- You are protective.
- You challenge others to want more for themselves.
- You are fearless.
- You are capable.
- You are charismatic.
- You turn heads when you walk into a room.
- You are confident.
- You are self-reliant.
- You have a giant heart paired with so much strength.

It's important that you know the goal isn't to not be a type eight. You don't need to reject everything that you are—even your strengths. It's simply about holding the awareness for what is keeping you away from your essence. It's OK that your good qualities are part of your type pattern—it doesn't make them less good.

Take some time to write out your personal strengths below.

_____

_____

_____

_____

_____

OPEN YOUR EYES TO BLIND SPOTS

This is the section where we run through all of the things that you will want to hold space for while you grow—the things that are habitual but aren't truly serving you in the pursuit of a life where you get to fully express your truest essence. In this, I want to let you know that a couple of these are going to be in direct contradiction to how you've traditionally viewed the world. It may, quite frankly, piss you off. But know that I write these things in love, and that I didn't make them up. (They're integrated ancient Enneagram teachings.) You are in the driver's seat of your growth journey—at the end of the day you decide how much of this is right for you.

For type eights who are familiar with the Enneagram, you've likely had people jam your blind spots down your throat. For whatever reason, I think type eights are often the most antagonized in the Enneagram. What's interesting is that if we want to support our type eights in tapping into their essence, banging them over the head with what we think is wrong with them really isn't the answer. Most eight-type patterns are formed out of the full self-acceptance of their flaws, especially when they are being asked to change to make others more comfortable. So my approach to this is less "Here's what you should change for us," and more "Here are some things that aren't serving you in the long run."

A few things to keep in mind as a type eight:

1. Power doesn't equal impact.
There's an important distinction to be made between power and influence. Power is the authority to make others do what you want them to do, while influence is the ability to impact the thoughts and beliefs of others through example instead of force.

It can be tempting, as a type eight who deeply desires not to be controlled, to choose a path of power, where they assert their preferences and will on those who surround them.

However, the type eights who truly thrive are the ones who take the path of influence—the eights who live a life so full of passion and belief and action that those in their circle can't help but be influenced. This is the beautiful strength of an aware type eight.

Type eights have the option to choose the path of purpose followed so boldly that it inspires those around them to walk the walk versus the empty attempts at asserting their power over the will of others.

2. You aren't invincible, and that's OK.

Type eights tend to push themselves to the limits in every single area of life—pushing through pain in order to get to the next level, staying up late and waking up early to accomplish a goal, or hiding their vulnerability as a way to prevent expressing weakness.

You—like all of us—are human. You have limits to your resources, and they will run out and lead to consequences, such as broken bones and torn ligaments, hospitalization, loss of relationships, and more.

Those consequences may be the one thing most type eights are not prepared to handle—the idea of being completely dependent upon others to make it through. Start balancing out your activities now. Notice when you're doing more than you have to do and when you're pushing yourself past your own limits. Take note of when you are trying to prove to yourself that you are strong, and use that time to prove to yourself instead that you are strong in willpower to resist that temptation.

3. Vulnerability will change your life.
There is likely nothing more important for type eights to learn than this. Take time to truly open up to someone or a few people. Be one hundred percent vulnerable with your fears, emotions, and childhood wounds.

This is like the express lane to personal growth for type eights. The place where you can admit your weakness is where you meet the part of yourself that has transcended your type pattern and stepped into your essence. Essentially, this is the shit.

I know it's not an easy ask and it's going to be uncomfortable in the beginning. But pick someone you feel safe with, and next time you find yourself wanting to argue or defend, take time to ask yourself what's really happening beneath that—what are you trying to hide? Express that instead of the argument, and see what happens!

4. Honesty without kindness is brutality.
Like I mentioned earlier, one of my favorite things about type eights is how direct and honest you are. I think this saves time, makes things clear, and keeps things simple. This is an amazing gift. However, there are a couple of ways that this can go wrong:

You have your idea of what is true, but it may not be the same as the person you're talking to. Be aware that you tend to value your own worldview over that of others. Because of this, you may say something that to you is "truth" but to another is rude. The reason this matters is that you end up forming unnecessary enemies and causing damage where it wasn't necessary.

When you share honesty without kindness, you create unwarranted trauma. Be intentional about checking your intentions. Do you feel expansive at the thought of sharing that truth, or do you feel contracted or vindicated? Know why you are taking the time to be "honest" with someone. Are you doing this for the good of the group, or are you doing it as a way to avoid your own vulnerability, feel more powerful, or receive vindication? Motives matter when sharing truth with people. When we approach truth with impure intentions, we end up inflicting more trauma on the world and cause more strife and unrest for ourselves in the process.

Of course, you're angry. You're exhausted. Type eights get a bad rep for being "angry" and volatile. While at times that may be true, I think it's important to recognize how much energy you are expending in all areas of your life. You are likely overworking, over-exercising, overindulging, and, in the process, in constant awareness of the potential of being betrayed or losing your role as leader—all while holding your own sadness, pain, and fear to yourself while feeling responsible for those you love. That's exhausting!

Do you know what happens to all of us when we are freaking exhausted? We become increasingly sensitive, quick-tempered, and impatient. Of course, there is work to do around not seeking thrill through conflict. But I also believe step one is finding ways to recognize when you're overdoing things so that in your bones you are more relaxed, rested, and at ease.

NOTE YOUR SUPPORT PLAN

This is the part of the process where we get to talk about finding what actually serves YOU when it comes to creating a life that you love. This is very exciting for me to share with type eights because often they are so busy doing that they forget to slow down and really listen. They often feel like they have to meet change and growth with strength—powering through what they need to improve.

So, how do we learn to allow ourselves grace and softness? For our type eights, I encourage you to start by regularly asking yourself this simple question: "Is there an easier way to do this?"

Below, you will find a list of things that may support you in the process of softening, opening, and finding balance.

A few things that may support you in the process:
- Develop a regular yoga and meditation practice.
- Choose a cause outside of yourself to put your excess energy behind.
- Take time to write out what balance would offer you in life. Be practical about it. Focus less on the way it would make you feel or what you know balance is supposed to offer you. Instead, be direct about what it would really provide for you in terms of life satisfaction.
- Keep a vulnerability journal or note in your phone—somewhere where you put your deepest fears, heartaches, and insecurities. If you don't want to risk someone finding them, feel free just to write them out and light them on fire.
- Practice the art of doing nothing. Take time just to exist without doing. Who are you when you don't have a role to play?
- Develop a creative practice, somewhere where you go just to play and express and make.
- Spend time with children and/or animals on a regular basis.
- Make it a habit to regularly volunteer your time to those in need. Intentionally place your focus on the needs of others.

What can you do this week to contribute to your life?

EXPLORE YOUR RELATIONSHIPS

So far, you've honored your strengths, gotten really honest with yourself about your blind spots, and set aside a plan of support in the process. Now it's time to talk about relationships. It's all well and good to do all of this work on our own, but what do we do when someone else comes in and they disrupt our perfect synchronicity of self-compassion? This is where we get to explore what you bring into your relationships. What do you positively contribute? What do you do that doesn't serve your work toward being the big-hearted, compassionate leader that you are in your essence?

Beautiful things that type eights bring to their relationships:
- Decisiveness.
- Protectiveness.
- Competence and capability.
- Showing us how much we're capable of.
- Being a great provider.
- Being fun to spend time with.
- Making us feel safe.

A few things that may not be serving your relationships:
- Constant defensiveness.
- Not opening up to reveal your humanity and share your burdens.
- Seeking constant intensity, which can lead to picking fights.
- Impatience with the weakness of others.
- Not letting others take the lead—particularly when your needs are in conflict with theirs.
- Overworking and neglect relationships.
- Demanding loyalty to you while not always exhibiting loyalty yourself.

The reason we're talking about this—even if it's uncomfortable and sometimes painful—is because, in the long run it will bring you so much relief. Holding the truth that both of these lists exist simultaneously is the key to ease in your relationships. Knowing what you can control and what isn't yours to worry about can be an extremely relaxing move to make. That tiny list up there, that's it. Think about that! You are doing so much right!

Take a few minutes to think of your own lists. Write down what you personally bring to your relationships, both positively and negatively.

Now, take a few moments here to think of the three most important relationships in your life. Write out how you would like for them to feel. How would they change if you could imagine a world where they were exactly as you hoped?

What about your lists would need to shift in order to have the relationships that you want?

SOFTEN YOUR PATH

OK, so we've established what makes you amazing. (Way to go, by the way!) We've covered what areas of your life may be in need of some tender love and care. We've even discussed how to support yourself in this growth. Let's now talk about how we're going to keep this process going, even when it feels difficult or impossible or a bit too unnatural.

I want to give you these four soft internal shifts to make—just four things to hold on to each and every day that will help you in the work of being your healthiest type eight self.

1. Focus on finding peace versus changing your behavior.
We both know that you can be very rebellious, so it's not always helpful to add a bunch of rules for yourself. It can simply make you want to just tell them to bug off. Instead of trying to magically be less defensive or not seek control, I suggest that you focus on bringing in more peace—finding opportunities to practice mindfulness through meditation, yoga, or even quiet afternoons at home by yourself. Take time to slow down and be intentionally peaceful. At the end of the day, you need to feel rested in order to reduce your autopilot desire to defend yourself.

2. Add in vulnerability.
In the same way, look for opportunities to share the truth beneath the truth—the real reason you are feeling protective, defensive, or rebellious. Share what you're scared of, what you're worried about, or if you're sad. If you aren't yet ready to do this with another human, start with just writing it down. Then eventually take it to the streets and share with those who matter the most to you. There's so much opening and healing that can happen when you allow others in and see how they love you anyway.

3. Know your "why" and deal with your childhood.
Start getting to know yourself really well. Why do you feel protective of yourself? What threat are you defending against? What does having control of a situation offer your inner child? Why did you pick a fight just now?

Get curious! Get especially curious about where in childhood you learned that you were on your own. Was there an early betrayal? A lack of safety? A feeling of being rejected by your family of origin? What happened and how has that impacted the way you walk through the world?

4. Give time and energy to a cause you care about.

When type eights really get behind a cause, they can make incredible things happen! In the same way that it's important for you to do this for the greater good, it's also important that you do this for you. Taking the time to use your skill set for the benefit of other people puts you in the mindset of the healthiest version of who you are. This is a fast track to your essence. Be mindful, though, that entering into this work doesn't absolve you from doing the work of releasing your type pattern. Being unnecessarily defensive, aggressive, and hurtful on behalf of a cause isn't healing—it's moving your focus of attention. True healing will come through doing all of these steps together.

TURN THAT INTO SOMETHING BEAUTIFUL

Creativity is important for all types. But having a creative outlet is important for type eights in their process of returning to essence. Taking the time to do something without a purpose and just for the sake of creating will help you get out of your normal pattern of pushing through and working hard. It will give you a place to go that is focused more on lightness, play, and vulnerable expression.

So what do you as a type eight need to keep in mind when it comes to creativity?

- Be cautious of making it another chore. Focus more on this being a place for mindfulness and play.
- Play with how vulnerable you can be with what you're making.
- Explore several outlets until you find the one that makes you feel the most free and inspired.
- Make yourself wait before attempting to turn this into a business. That's not the original point. That may end up being a great outcome. But focus on why you're doing this (to create a space of freedom, rest, and playfulness in your life).

- Be mindful of neglecting relationships in favor of your hobby and neglecting your hobby in favor of relationships. This is another opportunity to practice balance.
- You may need to do things that feel "frivolous" or "pointless'" in order to get your creative juices flowing. Allow yourself to take your creativity process seriously. It's worthy of your attention just like anything else in your life. Sometimes, to feel our most creative, we need to put ourselves in the path of inspiration. That may look like going to movies, visiting art galleries, going to see live music, etc.

~~~~~~~~

Dear Eight

I want to first issue an apology on behalf of Enneagram culture. I think we've done you a disservice by seeing you strictly in your type pattern and forgetting to know your essence.

When you're strong, it's hard for others to push through and look for the vulnerability there. I can't imagine the loneliness felt in the moments when you're tired, scared, and overburdened. The act of hiding your weakness from people in your life may temporarily shield them from your burden, but it also shields you from receiving the love that you are worthy of throughout your life. That same hole that you keep plugging up to prevent new wounds from forming, that's the same outlet through which you can let in love, and it's preventing your incredible capacity to love others from getting out.

I know it feels like peeling your skin off to share your weakness with others, but the skin underneath is tender whether you allow someone to soothe it or not.

It takes so much work to stay protected.

I beg of you to rest. Take the time you need to bring in peace, release your defensive stance, and open up your incredible heart to the people who are waiting in the wings, ready to love you.

You deserve rest, safety, and true soul nourishment.

And the world is begging for you to show up in your essence, because when you do, it's one of the most remarkable things the world gets to see. Take time to honor your negative emotions and you'll find that you move through them with much more ease and, ultimately, will need much less stimulation to maintain your naturally joyful spirit!

HEALER

PEACEMAKER

COMFORTER

SECRET GURU

Type Nine

"I know that I will be OK as long as those around me are OK."

BINGO

Waits to speak until they have something to say	"I feel like all the types."	Not really an introvert, but kind of.	Secretly meets people's needs and never gets credit	Always knows whose turn it is to speak
Netflix & chill.	Cozy AF.	Procrastination.	"Just tell me step by step how to do it."	Pizza.
Favorite blanket.	Naps.	9	"Have you thought about their perspective?"	"I don't want to offend anyone."
Quietly stubborn.	Finally expresses their opinion . . . no one hears	"Is that selfish of me?"	"That sounds stressful."	Loves being home
"Yeah, I can do that."	The woods.	Headphones.	Autonomy.	"I'm fine with whatever."

WHEN YOU GET A TATTOO

By Enneagram type.

1 - GETS TATTOO - ISN'T QUITE PLEASED WITH IT. THINKS ABOUT IT OFTEN.

2 - ACCIDENTALLY GETS TATTOO FACING OUTWARD SO THAT OTHERS CAN READ IT BUT IT'S ALWAYS UPSIDE DOWN FOR THEM.

3 - HAS A PINTEREST BOARD WITH ALL OF THEIR FAVORITE TATTOO IDEAS - WHETHER THEY GET A TATTOO OR NOT.

4 - GETS TATTOO - SEES SOMEONE ELSE WITH THE SAME TATTOO - DIES A LITTLE INSIDE.

5 - DOES A TON OF RESEARCH TO FIGURE OUT WHERE THE BEST PLACE TO GET IT WOULD BE AS WELL AS WHICH INKS ARE LEAST LIKELY TO FADE.

6 - GETS A MATCHING TATTOO WITH THEIR BEST FRIEND FROM KINDERGARTEN.

7 - NO, THANK YOU - THAT'S TOO BIG OF A COMMITMENT. OR "LET'S GET TATTOOS TONIGHT!" NO IN-BETWEEN.

8 - GETS A TATTOO IN THE MOST PAINFUL POSSIBLE PLACE AND DOESN'T FLINCH ONCE.

9 - EVERYONE IN YOUR LIFE IS SHOCKED THAT YOU GOT A TATTOO EVEN THOUGH IT DOESN'T FEEL VERY OUT OF CHARACTER TO YOU.

@enneagramandcoffee

ABOUT TYPE NINE

Basic Desire: "It's important to me that I maintain my peace of mind."

Basic Fear: "I worry about creating rifts with people in my life that cannot be repaired."

Type nines are empathetic, easygoing, and peaceful. In childhood, type nines learned that the best way to keep the peace was to minimize their own presence. They absorbed the idea that if they were to speak up and ask for what they need, then they would just be creating more problems. This can lead to a lifetime of learning to merge their desires with the needs of the room—a practice that ultimately makes type nines quite likable but also disconnected from a deep understanding of who they really are and what they want.

Type nines are conscientious, adaptable, selfless, and likely the most likable person you know.

I titled type nines "Secret Gurus" because I believe type nines are grossly underestimated by most of the people in their lives. While type nines can be slow to insert themselves and their opinions, it doesn't mean that they don't have them. In fact, because type nines spend so much time in their awareness of other people, they are often full of rich wisdom and insight that carries the perspectives of everyone. When a type nine takes the steps to speak out and share their opinion, it's really important that the rest of us make a point to listen. There is so much gold in the minds and hearts of our type nines.

Most types nines possess all elements of the Enneagram. The organization of a one, the helpfulness and consideration of a type two, the empathy of a type four, the playfulness of a type seven, etc. This gives them the unique perspective of being able to truly understand the worldview of every type. This can often make it difficult for type nines to type themselves. They see themselves in every type except for the type nine. This happens to be one of their consistent struggles in life—the finding of who they truly are outside of the world around them.

Many type nines have spent their entire lives doing everything they can to make the world around them work more smoothly—bending, swaying, not interjecting, and asking questions, all in service of keeping peace in their environment. One of the main reasons this happens is because the type nine craves peace of mind themselves, and when there is conflict in the environment, there is less ability for them to maintain their own personal peace of mind.

Type nines value comfort and ease. They tend to be homebodies (although not always) and appreciate the comfort that can be found in their familiar environments. A lot of time, type nines have a desire to "cozify" their space with blankets, candles, and other comfort items. They may enjoy hobbies that are relaxing in nature, like television and puzzles, and occasionally type nines are nap enthusiasts.

This doesn't mean that our type nines aren't quite busy. In fact, they spend a lot of energy and time doing things for other people and can accidentally overcommit themselves. They may also busy themselves with projects that will help to bring them more comfort and peace of mind in the long run.

SUBTYPES OF TYPE NINE

The following subtypes of type nine are based on the three instinctual variants and how those interact with the type nine's pattern of merging. The self-preservation type nine merges through physical comforts, the social type nine merges with groups of people, and the sexual type nine merges with individuals.

SELF-PRESERVATION

- Seeks physical comfort
- Appreciates routine
- Concrete people who don't relate as much to abstract ideas or concepts
- Wants more alone time than the other subtypes
- Cheerful and fun-loving
- Possesses a stronger presence than the other two subtypes
- More inclined toward a lavish lifestyle
- More likely to be stubborn or irritable

SOCIAL

- Prioritizes the group's needs above his or her own
- Overly generous with resources to please the needs of the group
- Has a deep desire to belong to the group and will do whatever it takes to fit in
- Can be a workaholic
- Very outgoing and energetic
- Gives of themselves unconditionally
- Can be mistaken for a type two or three

SEXUAL

- Merges inside of relationships
- Can lack a sense of structure and certainty that they seek through other people
- The least assertive of the subtypes
- May be so focused on meeting the needs of others that he or she neglects his or her own needs

TYPE NINE AND WINGS

As a type nine, you can pull from either of your wings to help round out your personality. You may find that you already lean in one direction more than the other. However, you have access to the skills and vices of both wings. Here are some qualities you can borrow from your neighbors:

TYPE EIGHT WING

Using this wing can aid you in being more direct and upfront about what you need. It can aid you in setting healthy boundaries and communicating directly instead of passive-aggressively. It can also aid you in developing leadership skills and pushing through difficult tasks.

TYPE ONE WING

This wing can help you create discipline and structure for yourself. It can also aid you in developing your vision for an ideal world—a strong sense of right and wrong that uses your skills of mediation and the strong ethics of your one wing to become an effective humanitarian.

TYPE NINE AND LINES

When in stress, the type nine moves to type six, and when in rest, they move to type three. With that understanding, here's what you may want to keep in mind in your relationship to stress and self-care.

RECOGNIZING YOUR STRESS

When stressed out, type nines may find themselves in the lower end of type six. This can look like entering into worst-case scenario thinking, committing for too long to relationships that aren't serving the type nine, intensely worrying about projects and work problems, and finally becoming increasingly passive-aggressive. In this state, the type nine may avoid looking at the ways in which they contribute to their own unhappiness, focusing instead on the behavior of others.

SELF-CARE INFUSION

When you start to notice this come up in you, you have the tools you need to care for yourself. Using the high side of type three, you can take the time to prioritize who you are and what you want. You can take the time to put yourself out there creatively and socially and let others know what you bring to the table. You can use this move as a way to increase your energy for projects and push through the initial discomfort of doing what needs to be done to reach a point of success.

RECOGNIZING STAGNATION

In the same way that you can use the high side of type three, you can also accidentally slip into the lower levels of this type. This can look like frantically doing tasks as a way to feel like you're making up for what hasn't been done—the same kind of energy you experience when you've slept through your alarm and need to get ready in five minutes. Approaching work in this way only increases your self-doubt and keeps you busy with unnecessary tasks.

MOTIVATION INFUSION

This is where it's helpful to bring in the high side of type six. In this way, you can choose to be proactive in the pursuit of your personal goals—making small moves over time that add up to a larger achievement. You can also use the analytical side of six to get clear on who you are, what you want, and where you'd like to go.

LEVELS OF HEALTH

HEALTHY
In their healthiest state, type nines become self-aware, self-possessed, and present. They are able to recognize that their presence matters and, through that, achieve peace of mind that is not circumstantial. They are great mediators, servant leaders, and inspiring creators.

AVERAGE
In most cases, our type nines are fearful of conflict in their lives. They take great efforts to avoid conflict through merging, numbing out, and being a people pleaser. They are uncomfortable with discomfort, which can keep them from pursuing great goals past the point that is feels easy for them. They downplay their desires, hurt feelings, and needs in relationships as a way to prevent disruption in their peace of mind.

UNHEALTHY
The type nine may refuse to deal with the reality of conflict at all—denying, suppressing, and dissociating. This can lead the type nine to become increasingly numb to his or her life and closed off to the desires of the heart. In extreme cases, the type nine may even stop responding altogether.

GETTING H.O.N.E.S.T. FOR TYPE NINE

What I believe is remarkable about type nines is the way that they have mastered the art of perspective. Being able to hold space for other people, exactly as they are, can create a safe place to land for many. Type nines are probably the most liked type on the Ennea-gram. I don't think this is merely because they strive to make others comfortable but also because they have high standards of acceptance for people as they are, letting people have their turn and not speaking unless the type nine has something to contribute. Because of this, I believe type nines make the most incredible leaders. In fact, they are the people I want training our leaders how to be leaders. Once a type nine pushes through the initial discomfort of stepping into authority, they lead in such a way that truly takes humanity into account. They're thoughtful, inquisitive, and able to hold space for conflicting needs among their team. It's a beautiful thing to witness.

What is equally heartbreaking for me is that all of this wisdom, magic, and insight can go completely unseen by both type nines and those around them. Until our type nines take the time to truly get to know who they are outside of the world around them and what they're passionate about and feel safe to share their honest thoughts and feelings, they may go through life being present but not seen. In addition, even after our type nines become comfortable with openly sharing their thoughts with those they're closest to, there can be a disconnect with the drive to do more with who they are. They may lose themselves in performing tasks for other people or in the comfort and safety of not doing more than what they've already done. There is so much wisdom in the world that is being completely kept secret because there are type nines who are fearful of leaving their comfort zones.

HONOR YOUR STRENGTHS

The first step is to take time to get really honest with yourself about what makes you amazing. Celebrate all of the elements of your personality that you love. If it's tricky for you to think of things you love about yourself, consider what you do and who you are that contributes positively to the world around you.

A few things that are amazing about type nines:

- You are inclusive.
- You are considerate.
- You ask good questions.
- You are non-judgmental.
- You are easy to be around.
- You are a safe place to land.
- You are easygoing.
- You are grounded and stable.
- You make others feel comfortable in your presence.
- You offer us perspective.
- You are kind.
- You have so much wisdom to share with us.

It's important that you know the goal isn't to not be a type nine. You don't need to reject everything that you are—even your strengths. It's simply about holding the awareness for what is keeping you away from your essence. It's OK that your good qualities are part of your type pattern—it doesn't make them less good.

Take some time to write out your personal strengths below.

_____

_____

_____

_____

_____

OPEN YOUR EYES TO BLIND SPOTS

This is the section where we run through all of the things that you will want to hold space for while you grow—the things that are habitual but aren't truly serving you in the pursuit of a life where you get to fully express your truest essence. In this, I want to let you know that a couple of these are going to be in direct contradiction to how you've traditionally viewed the world. It may, quite frankly, piss you off. But know that I write these things in love, and that I didn't make them up. (They're integrated ancient Enneagram teachings.) You are in the driver's seat of your growth journey—at the end of the day you decide how much of this is right for you.

For a lot of types, we're focusing on how not to harm other people with less-than-healthy behavior patterns. For type nines, we're going to be putting a lot more focus on how you are silencing yourself and keeping yourself small. There is so much that the world wants and needs to learn from our type nines. My hope is that this chapter helps you to be a more honest version of who you are both with yourself and others.

A few things to keep in mind as a type nine:

1. Conflict is normal, and you will survive it.
There is so much in your life that will go more smoothly if you let this digest. The willingness to sit with conflict will lead to more healthy relationships, meaningful work opportunities, and experiences that bring you to life.

The first time Shelly had an argument in her marriage, she thought that it was the end. It took years of practice to remain in that discomfort and push through to the other side of what ended up being the richest emotional experience of their marriage.

2. We want to hear what you have to say.
The people in your life care about what you have to say. We want to hear your ideas, thoughts, and experiences. Here's where I think a

lot of type nines get tripped up—the interjection. Most people in a conversation are volunteering information, even if it's not being asked for. Most type nines are extremely conscientious about not inserting themselves or stirring the pot. This can mean that conversation after conversation could go by without the type nine ever expressing an idea or opinion that wasn't directly requested. The thing to learn here is that we want to hear you. We value that you're there. Most people aren't aware of the need to ask you directly to share your thoughts and opinions. It's OK to interject and just share without a good reason—people want to know you and that's enough.

3. Stop saying "yes" right away.
There can often be a bit of an automatic response when someone asks a type nine for help—just a "yes" that slips out of the mouth without much thought or effort. For the most part, this happens because type nines are relatively easygoing and eager to please. But sometimes this happens when it directly conflicts with your personal needs or even responsibilities. Take the time to say, "Let me think about it and get back to you." This will give you the time and space that you need to think over if it's really something you want to do and express your "no" with a bit more distance.

4. You will make it to the other side of discomfort.
So many of our greatest teachers never shared their thoughts with the world because they wouldn't push through discomfort. When things get sticky and you're forced to do something you've never done before or haven't even learned how to do yet, you will make it through. Everything in life is figure-out-able, and no feeling will last forever. You can push through that temporary moment of uneasiness and make it to the other side safe, sound, and more accomplished.

5. You're not lazy—you're overextended.

One of my least favorite stereotypes of the Enneagram is the idea that type nines are lazy. The idea that anyone is lazy at all is offensive to me. When most people are said to be "lazy," it's usually because of a lack of prioritizing, a fear of putting themselves out there, unaddressed sadness, or what I believe is ultimately the case with our type nines—being overextended in their lives.

I know that a lot of type nines are reading this thinking, "I don't know, I don't do that much throughout the day," while others are already really busy and relating to this on a scheduling level. What I mean by overextended is much less in terms of time and more in terms of mental energy. You're spending all day, every day, hyperaware of the needs and emotional temperatures of other people. You see someone subtly alter their facial expression, and you go grab them a chair. Someone asks you how you feel about the restaurant across the street, and you go to great lengths to give the most diplomatic answer you can. You are expending far more energy than the average person just to exist as you are.

That's why I'm not going to tell you to get off the couch in this section or to stop watching that TV show you love (because honestly, who cares?). What I'm going to encourage you to do is take the risk of pissing off more people. Just save yourself that energy and don't bend and sway to the perceived desires of strangers throughout a given day. Play with what it feels like to exist as you are without making it cozy for everyone else—just for a day, and then maybe a week.

NOTE YOUR SUPPORT PLAN

This is the part of the process where we get to talk about finding what actually serves YOU when it comes to creating a life that you love. This is very exciting for me to share with type nines because they are often so focused on not making waves and ensuring that others feel comfortable and safe that they can feel unclear about their own wants and needs.

So, how do we learn to listen to ourselves and speak up when we have things to share? For our type nines, I encourage you to start by spending more time alone. Specifically, alone time out of your house. Get used to making decisions that cannot impact anyone else. Bring that energy and decisiveness with you when you are in experiences with others as well.

Below, you will find a list of things that may support you in the process of being more upfront about who you are, feeling understood by the people in your life, and getting more of yourself out into the world.

A few things that may support you in the process:
- Find a method for prioritizing. Check in each month, week, and morning, and get clear with yourself about what really needs to take place in that time frame to achieve what you'd like to achieve.
- Practice speaking up on the small things—choose the place you eat for dinner, pick the music in the car, etc. Build the habit in the small things.
- Many type nines benefit from a relationship to the outdoors. Getting in nature and moving your body can greatly connect you to your purpose and bring you true feelings of peace.
- Adopt a way of moving your body that pushes you to go through your discomfort, such as a group exercise class or a buddy program where you feel the pressure not to give up.
- Wake up earlier and give yourself a luxurious morning routine. This will get you up and at 'em sooner and give you plenty of time to have a nice, slow, intentional start to the day.

- Find a place to share your words. Whether through a blog, social media, or a storytelling event in your area, find an outlet for putting your thoughts out into the world.
- Play with the idea of writing an opinion piece for your local newspaper. Choose a topic and write a letter to the editor about your thoughts on the situation. You don't have to send it in, just take the time to get really honest with yourself about what you think.
- Make it a habit to say "Let me think about it" when asked to give of your time and energy. Make sure you're only agreeing to do something when it truly does feel right for you.

What can you do this week to contribute to your life?

EXPLORE YOUR RELATIONSHIPS

So far, you've honored your strengths, gotten really honest with yourself about your blind spots, and set aside a plan of support in the process. Now it's time to talk about relationships. It's all well and good to do all of this work on our own, but what do we do when someone else comes in and they disrupt our perfect synchronicity of self-compassion? This is where we get to explore what you bring into your relationships. What do you positively contribute? What do you do that doesn't serve your work to being the big-hearted, compassionate leader that you are in your essence.

Beautiful things that type nines bring to their relationships:
- Being considerate.
- Kindness.
- Reminders to be selfless.
- Being a great sounding board.
- Supportiveness.
- Sharing your insight.
- Being a safe place to be ourselves.

A few things that may not be serving your relationships:
- Merging with the opinions of others in a relationship.
- Sacrificing too much.
- Stubborn and passive-aggressive.
- Settling for not getting your needs met.
- Losing yourself inside of your relationships.
- Checking out mentally at the first sign of conflict.
- Not taking the extra steps to make people feel special to you through romantic gestures or thoughtful contributions.

The reason we're talking about this—even if it's uncomfortable and sometimes painful—is because, in the long run it will bring you so much relief. Holding the truth that both of these lists exist simultaneously is the key to ease in your relationships. Knowing what you can control and what isn't yours to worry about can be an extremely relaxing move to make. That tiny list up there, that's it. Think about that! You are doing so much right!

Take a few minutes to think of your own lists. Write down what you personally bring to your relationships, both positively and negatively.

Now, take a few moments here to think of the three most important relationships in your life. Write out how you would like for them to feel. How would they change if you could imagine a world where they were exactly as you hoped?

What about your lists would need to shift in order to have the relationships that you want?

SOFTEN YOUR PATH
OK, so we've established what makes you amazing. (Way to go, by the way!) We've covered what areas of your life may be in need of

some tender love and care. We've even discussed how to support yourself in this growth. Let's now talk about how we're going to keep this process going even when it feels difficult or impossible or a bit too unnatural.

I want to give you these four soft internal shifts to make—just four things to hold on to each and every day that will help you in the work of being your healthiest type nine self.

1. Spend more time out alone doing things.
It's important for type nines to take time away from others to see what they truly love doing. What kind of food do you enjoy? What kind of activities make you happy? What would you do if no one were impacted by your decisions? This will help you get more intimate with your identity and preferences so that it's easier to share them over time.

2. Focus on knowing your priorities.
One of the biggest struggles our type nines can experience is with the ability to truly prioritize. When looking at a list of tasks, everything seems equally important and, therefore, equally overwhelming. Taking the time to set your priorities each month will aid you in creating a filter through which to run opportunities and tasks. If your priority is finishing a quilt, then ask yourself, "Will this task help me get closer to finishing my quilt?" If not, let it go. If your priority is spending time with your children, ask yourself, "Will this task give me more or less time to spend with my kids?"

3. Do something "hard" every week.
It's important for our type nines to practice building muscle—not necessarily physically, but mentally—by building up the habit of pushing through uncomfortable steps in the process. I encourage type nines

to do one hard thing each week, something that pushes you out of your comfort zone and past what you think you're capable of.

4. Start to view hiding yourself as lying to people you care about.
This may seem really intense, but that's what we're doing when we're not open with others about who we are. We're lying to them. We're playing a role that makes them comfortable with us without having to be open and vulnerable ourselves. We convince them we're what they want us to be and create a dynamic not built on honest connection, but instead on hiding who we are. Next time you consider hiding who you are to make others comfortable, ask yourself if you feel OK lying to them and choose radical honesty instead.

TURN THAT INTO SOMETHING BEAUTIFUL

Creativity is important for all types. But having a creative outlet is important for type nines because it can be such a great way to get to know yourself, experience a comforting and peaceful outlet, and allow you to find things that you truly love doing.

So what do you as a type nine need to keep in mind when it comes to creativity?
- Break it up into tiny, bite-sized pieces; do the tiniest first step, and go from there.
- Everything is Google-able. If you don't know how to do it yet, you can always find out. There are great resources, like tutorials on YouTube and Skillshare, or you can always take a class.
- Make sure that you're doing something that is yours and not the interest of a partner or close friend. This is your creative expression, not an extension of theirs.
- There is no wrong or right way to be creative—just do stuff and see what happens.

- If you're not sure how you'd like to get creative or what outlet interests you, just start doing things. Don't try to figure it out in your mind, just do one thing this week and see how it feels. Then try something else next week, until you find one thing you want to keep doing.

~~~~~~~~~~

Dear Nine

Thank you for being who you are in the world. Thank you for your kindness, awareness of other people, and willingness to take us as we are. Thank you for your comforting presence and for being such a safe place to be exactly who we are with you.

We are ready and willing to be that for you as well. We crave more of your mind, and your presence here matters. We ache to know who you truly are and to connect with the essence of what you bring to the table.

You are incredible and needed in your relationships and in our society.

You are wise. You are kind. You are loved, and your presence here matters so deeply!

CONCLUSION

I know that you've likely digested A LOT at this point about who you are, why you operate the way you do, and how that impacts the world around you. For that, I want to say, "Thank you." Taking the time to learn how and why you engage with the world the way you do is the kind of good work that creates a ripple into the atmosphere.

The tenderness and compassion with which you approach yourself turns into tenderness and compassion for your partner, your mother, your barista, etc., which can bleed into the tenderness and compassion that they can show themselves, to others, and so on.

This work you are doing, this awareness-seeking, is good work, and not just for you—for the world. So thank you for creating one more ripple of kindness in the universe.

It took me some time to figure out what I wanted to leave you with as you exit the care of these pages. What do you need to carry with you if all else fades from your memory?

I realize that more than anything I want to give you permission—permission to explore, to mess up, to try again, and to ask for what you need.

Life can be hard. We're all carrying these hefty, unique burdens, and our psyches have found interesting and unique ways to cope with the reality of being human. Some of us fill our time with fun activities, others make themselves small, and others try to plan for the worst-case scenarios. We are all different in the ways we cope, but the reality is that we are all coping.

You are doing the best you can with what you've been given, and that's OK. As you enter into this work, I want you to know that you will likely never surpass your type pattern. Instead, you will slip and get back up again and again and again.

I tell you this not to discourage you. Rather, I tell you this as a source of encouragement. You are normal. You are fine. You are human. Humans do not ever exceed their humanity. We simply find ways to do less harm and more good. As you move forward, I hope that you find gentleness with yourself and others in this process.

I hope that, when you fall, you are now able to recognize what happened and how to communicate it, all while holding awareness that, within all of this humanity, there are some truly incredible strengths.

I don't anticipate your perfection. I anticipate your process to remain a process.

I want to leave you with the seemingly hopeless—but actually hopeful—idea that you will never outgrow your Enneagram type.

I know it sounds depressing to some of you. But hear me out when I say that it's actually great news. The idea that we can and should outgrow ourselves is what causes self-abandonment in the moments when we deal with the "same old things," when in reality we should celebrate that we're catching them earlier and doing less harm each time.

The work of the Enneagram isn't about outgrowing who you are. Rather, it's about recognizing that it's not ALL that you are, that you don't need to lean on your personality as a way to get through the world, that you are safe, that you are loved, and that you are worthy without all of those mechanisms that you've developed over time.

If you're seeking a supportive community of like-minded individuals doing the work of the Enneagram, I encourage you to join us over at www.enneagramandcoffee.com. We are building a beautiful community of people who are truly changing the world from the inside out.

Enjoy *The Honest Enneagram* as an audiobook, wherever audiobooks are sold.